# I'M NOT OKAY WITH GRAY

How To Create An Extraordinary Life After 50

BY
COACH MICHAEL TAYLOR

I'm Not Okay With Gray

Published by Creation Publishing Group LLC
www.creationpublishing.com
© 2022 Michael Taylor
ISBN # 978-1-7366369-6-1
Library of Congress Number # 2022902290

All rights reserved. No part of this book may be used, reproduced, stored in, introduced into a retrieval system, or transmitted in any form or by any means without the express written consent of the publisher. Published and printed in the United States of America.

# Contents

Foreword ................................................................................v

Acknowledgments ..................................................................ix

Introduction ...........................................................................1

Chapter 1: Do Not Embrace A Midlife Crisis ...........................5

Chapter 2: Embrace Who You Are ........................................17

Chapter 3: Embrace Spirituality ............................................41

Chapter 4: Embrace Connection ...........................................57

Chapter 5: Embrace Health and Fitness ................................81

Chapter 6: Embrace Financial Abundance .............................93

Chapter 7: Embrace Joy, Passion, and Purpose ....................107

Chapter 8: Embrace Diversity .............................................129

Chapter 9: Embrace Technology .........................................147

Chapter 10: Embrace Being In Service ................................161

Bio .....................................................................................171

# Foreword

By Kevin Kitrell Ross
Senior Minister of Unity of Sacramento

As a frequent traveler, I enjoy meeting people from all walks of life. At times, I am people-watching. Other times, I am fortunate enough to be engaged in a conversation over a meal. Either way, I love meeting new people and learning how they see and experience the world and the interesting ways they are human.

On one such occasion, I was traveling back to the United States from Barcelona, Spain. I was not particularly in a talking mood. In fact, I was looking forward to a restful trip back to the US, where I undoubtedly would be facing an onslaught of excitement from my family and a week packed with meetings. Nevertheless, my business class seatmate was in a chatty mood, so I perked up and obliged him. After exchanging some pleasantries and learning a little about each other's careers, the conversation became interesting.

This jovial middle-aged Irish man came alive when he learned that I was a minister. He had a burning question in his heart that he wanted me to answer.

"Since you're a minister and all, riddle me this: 'Why is it that just when we reach an age in life where we have accrued enough money, material success, and worldly acclaim, God strikes you with sickness so that you spend the rest of your life, unable to really enjoy it?'"

This middle-aged, burly Irish man was desperately looking for an answer. He had become the caretaker for his ailing father, and he found it completely unfair that God would do this to His "children" that He claimed to love so much.

Suddenly, I felt a pressure to defend God. I felt a need to get God off of the hook as it became abundantly clear to me that this man's problem was not a God problem at all but a paradigm problem.

With a sense of mission and compassion, I said to my seatmate, "Your issue is not with God. Your issue is with a Westernized paradigm of aging. Our Western world glorifies youth and demonizes aging. It says to us, 'the younger you are, the better you are. The older you are, the more you should be trying to be younger, so you can be better.' Mass media equates youth with health and equates aging with sickness. Sir, you don't have a God problem. You have a paradigm problem."

I continued by sharing with him how the reverse is often true in many Eastern cultures. "The messages are completely opposite. Elders are revered, prized, and what every young person aspires to become. Becoming older is equated with becoming wiser. And the pursuit of wisdom is valued over the pursuit of things, and aging is not something to be feared but something to look forward to. Becoming an elder is an honored status. It is the one having this status who also knows the secrets to longevity, vitality and wholeness."

When I finished speaking, my new friend's eyes were lit up and actually welling up with tears of joy. He had never looked at it this way. He breathed a sigh of relief and thanked me for opening his eyes. I could see that he had an entirely new lease on life. I, too, breathed a sigh of relief for having gotten God off the proverbial hook.

With the definitions that have been promulgated and normalized about aging, it is no wonder why people view reaching their 50s as a crisis. This view of aging assumes that life is a declining bottomless pit of physical decay and social isolation. This view of aging is fear-based and filled with erroneous myths that I am happy my friend Michael Taylor is challenging head-on with this new book, "Not Ok with Gray."

What if we came to embrace a new paradigm that posits, "The

longer I live, the better I become at living?" What might open up in the quality of our lives if we abandoned the false notion that a calendar has any power to determine the health of our bodies, the sweetness of our relationships, the height of our achievement, the limit of our financial potential, or the extent of our legacy? In substance, this would be joining with my spiritual mentor, the late Reverend Dr. Johnnie Colemon, who declared, "Age is not of my spiritual business." Because of this, she achieved more than most would accomplish in ten lifetimes in her lifetime — simply because she did not let a calendar limit the heights in her skies.

Imagine what new possibilities might open up for living a life of purpose, passion, peace and prosperity if we were not afraid to move to the next stage of our development as humans. What if we could see each stage offering a new gift and each gift being more meaningful than the former? What if we are, in fact, not aging, but evolving? And with each evolutionary circuit around the sun, we are amassing a greater capacity to love, serve, heal, and transform the world in which we live? With this evolutionary paradigm, we move into each new stage of our journey, anticipating the best and enthused about getting there. Our disposition is regenerative, and we can see that the rest of our lives will be the best of our lives.

Fortunately, we don't have to imagine; Michael Taylor has laid it out in this book. All we have to do is take the journey. All aboard!!!

## Kevin Kitrell Ross

For over twenty-five years, Kevin Kitrell Ross has been on a mission to inspire people to awaken to their highest potential and be a force for good. This global mission has led him to serve people as an international keynote speaker, moderator, panelist, author, radio talk show host, master life coach and most prominently, the Senior Minister of Unity of Sacramento International Spiritual Center. He has earned a reputation as a respected bridge-building interfaith social justice activist who has shared the stage with luminaries ranging from Corretta Scott King, Rev. C.T. Vivian, Marianne Williamson, Deepak Chopra,

His Holiness, the Dalai Lama, President Nelson Mandela, and Vice President Kamala Harris.

He is an author of multiple books, including Breathing Space: A 52 Week Meditation Journey for Centered, Soulful and Successful Living and two Children's books. Rev. Kev. is a south side Chicago native, a graduate of Morehouse College, a three-time humanitarian award recipient, and an inductee into the Martin Luther King, Jr. International Clergy Hall of Honor at Morehouse. Among his highest honors was being invited to pray for the nation as he opened a session of the United States House of Representatives in Washington, DC. He is presently a student at Harvard Divinity School, earning his Master in Religion and Public Life degree.

Rev. Kev. is married to Anita Ross, founder of the Women for Equality movement, and together they have three children.

# Acknowledgments

FIRST, FOREMOST, AND always, I must acknowledge the Divine Energy and Intelligence that created and is still creating this amazing Universe we live in. Words cannot fully express the unadulterated joy I feel regularly due to the intimacy and connection I have with the Source of all things. As I reflect over the past 30 years or so of my life, I am in complete awe of the transformation I've gone through. Transforming from an Atheist to a person who is completely connected to his spiritual essence as a spiritual being is nothing short of a miracle. So, to the God of my understanding, I simply say thank you for this amazing gift called life. I can clearly see my divine purpose for being here at this unique time in history, and I have committed my life to be in service to you, and I will do everything in my power to work hand in hand with you in helping create heaven right here on earth.

---

Back in the early '90s, I came across a book by Deepak Chopra titled, Ageless Body, Timeless Mind. I was intrigued by the title, so I purchased it. Once I began reading it, I couldn't put it down. The book confirmed what I had always believed: that age is just a number, and there is a definite connection between longevity and spirituality. The book inspired me to embrace some new ideas about aging and introduced me to the understanding that science and spirituality can definitely coexist. The book laid the foundation for how I view aging and is partially responsible for me writing this particular book.

---

Bruce Lipton is a man that has shaped my views on the power of the human mind and how we can use it to create anything our heart desires. His book, The Biology of Belief, was instrumental in shaping my views and beliefs about the power each human being has in creating their own reality, and his teachings about the subconscious mind gave me a clear understanding of how to use my mind to create my version of an extraordinary life.

---

Louise Hay wrote a wonderful book titled, You Can Heal Your Life which literally helped me change my own life. Through her book, I learned how unhealed emotions could be responsible for physical ailments in the body, and by healing those emotions, you can heal your life. Through her book, I learned how repressing my anger caused me to have problems in my throat, and by addressing my repressed anger, I eliminated all of my throat problems.

---

Dr. Joe Dispenza is a man who has impacted my life in profound ways. Dr. Joe was hit by a vehicle and broke his back in several places, and was able to completely heal his back without surgery using meditation and his mind alone. Now he travels around the world teaching people how to access the Divine Intelligence within them to heal their bodies and create the life of their dreams. His teachings and meditations are powerful and transformational, and I highly recommend his book, Becoming Supernatural. In the book, he shares how you can heal your body using only the power of your mind and your thoughts, and he provides scientific evidence of how this is possible. The book is filled with case studies of ordinary people doing supernatural things, and once you read it, you will be inspired to become supernatural yourself.

---

I would be remiss if I didn't acknowledge the person who is primarily responsible for how I think. My mom Geneva is the person who taught me at a very young age if I wanted something badly enough, no one or no-thing could keep me from attaining it except myself. Thanks for all of the amazing lessons you taught me, mom.

---

And last but definitely not least, I must acknowledge the love of my life and one of my biggest supporters. My wife Bedra is my life partner who I get to share life with, and she loves and supports me in unimaginable ways. She believes in me as much as I believe in myself, and I am truly blessed to have her in my life. She is the absolute best wife I could have ever asked for.

---

Of course, I can't forget to acknowledge you, the reader, for picking up a copy of this book. If you're the type of person who would read a book like this, it tells me you're committed to living an extraordinary life, and I'm certain the insights contained in this book can help you on your journey. So jump right in and start creating the life you were born to live.

Enjoy!

# Introduction

On my 40th birthday, my son and I were on a road trip when he asked me if I felt old since I had just turned 40. Even though it's been twenty-one years since he asked me that question, I still remember it as though it were yesterday. What I remember most is the feeling I had as I answered the question. I remember a huge smile coming across my face, and I remember feeling happier than I had felt in a very long time. As I reflected on the question, I remember thinking about all the adversities I had overcome. Divorce, bankruptcy, foreclosure, depression, and homelessness. As I reflected on those experiences, I thought about how, despite those challenges, I was able to rebuild my life, and now I was happier than I had ever been.

I paused for a moment, and then said, "I'm not sure what being 40 is supposed to feel like, but to be completely honest, I definitely don't feel old. As a matter of fact, I feel like I'm still in my 20's.

My son looked at me and smiled, and then replied, " I guess I should have expected that answer from you because you are always pretty positive and optimistic."

Now that I'm in my 60's, I still feel the same way, maybe I no longer feel like I'm in my 20's physically, but for the most part, I still feel very young. Except for my knees (which do feel like 60-year-old knees from walking on concrete all day for more than 35 years), my body still feels young. I can do pretty much anything I want to physically and emotionally; I feel extremely optimistic, vibrant and energetic, and alive with passion and purpose.

I am absolutely convinced that life begins at 50, and with the right mindset and attitude, the second half of life can be much more rewarding and fulfilling than the first half.

This book intends to challenge you to embrace a new attitude about aging. Getting older does not mean a decline in your physical, intellectual, emotional, and spiritual wellbeing. It can be a process of becoming the best version of yourself, and it can be fun, joyful, rewarding and filled with passion and purpose.

So, if you're ready to experience life to the fullest, embrace the mantra, *I'm Not Okay With Gray*, which simply means you are unwilling to concede that life after 50 is supposed to be filled with struggle and challenges. Know that life was meant to be good, but no one said it would be easy.

My wish for you is that this book makes it a little easier for you!

Good luck!

*"Aging does not diminish my beauty
Never at any point does the universe give up on me, consider me not good enough, or consider me a has-been. Only if I think of myself in such ways do I block the flow of miracles into my life.*

*My value does not decline with my physical beauty. As my outer beauty begins to fade, my inner beauty shines forth most brightly. Spiritually, I am never invisible. I realize the light in each of us is the gorgeousness of the universe, no matter our age or physical condition. I live with humble gratitude for the light that shines within me. I will not be tempted by worldly thoughts that would hide from me my value. Aging does not diminish my beauty!"*

— **Marianne Williamson**

# CHAPTER 1
## Do Not Embrace A Midlife Crisis

WHILE DOING SOME research for this book, I ran across an article about midlife crisis on an online recovery website called 7 Summit Pathways. (www.7summitpathways.com) Here is an excerpt from the article:

The term "midlife crisis" has been around since the 1960s. It describes a normal transition that happens to both men and women during which you go from being a young person to an older adult. Usually, between the ages of 38 and 50, some individuals begin to struggle with the passing of their youth.

A midlife crisis can cause you to evaluate your life, achievements and dreams. Most people work their way through their midlife crisis without much trouble, quickly regaining balance. Others struggle with depression or anxiety as they face the next stage of their life.

### Signs and Symptoms of a Midlife Crisis

As you realize that you're getting older, it's completely normal to experience some mild unease or regret. Sadly, a midlife crisis can lead to dangerous side effects that can impact your emotional, physical and financial well-being. By understanding midlife crisis symptoms, you can feel more empowered to address them as they occur, including:

- Feeling stuck in a rut or hopeless about your options for the future
- Displaying dramatic changes in mood, such as irritability or anger
- Engaging in erratic or impulsive decision-making, such as purchasing big-ticket items like a new car
- Feeling the need for a new schedule, habit or challenge
- Oversleeping or experiencing the inability to sleep
- Obsessing over how you look and changing your personal appearance
- Disconnecting with old friends and replacing them with younger friends
- Changing career paths
- Leaving your spouse or committing infidelity
- Feeling listless or bored
- Experiencing bouts of depression, remorse or anxiety
- Entertaining obsessive thoughts about death or dying
- Increasing alcohol or drug use

As I read the article, I began reflecting on my own life and wanted to understand what actually causes a person to have a midlife crisis. I've concluded that a midlife crisis does not necessarily occur because of age. A midlife crisis is more like an internal knowing that something is missing in our lives, and we have no idea what it is. It is like our Souls' way of saying you aren't doing what you were put on the planet to do, and it feels like something is just not right in your life, and it is hard to put into words. It is an intuitive knowing that something is missing and you have no idea what it is.

I believe there are really only two things that will cause a person to want to change their lives to avoid a midlife crisis. The first thing is pain, and the other is divine discontent. These two things are the foundation of a midlife crisis.

In my case, my midlife crisis showed up as a result of experiencing a lot of pain. I experienced a series of adversities and challenges in my life. I went from living the American Dream at the age of 23 to watching that dream turn into the American nightmare at the age of 29. I went from having the house, the wife, the 2.5 kids and the 401K to being homeless for two years, living out of my car. As a result of those challenges, I began what I will call "my journey of transformation." My journey began with a miracle that changed the trajectory of my life and put me on a path of constant and never-ending improvement.

I was sitting up late one night because I was too depressed to sleep. I remember sitting at the edge of my bed, staring across the room at my bookshelf. As I stared at the books, I noticed that every book on my bookshelf had something to do with getting rich and making money. As I sat there staring at the books, all of a sudden, this question just popped into my mind. It was like a voiceless voice inside my head, but I heard it as clear as a bell. "Michael, what if you took all of the energy and effort you've used in trying to get rich and take that same energy to figure out how to be happy?"

It would be impossible to describe the feeling I had when I asked myself that question, but it literally changed and saved my life instantly. I wish I could fully explain it, but suddenly, my depression lifted, and I had this amazing clarity that my life was going to become extraordinary. At the time, my life was the complete opposite of that. I was about to be kicked out of my apartment, I was deeply in debt, I didn't have a job, I was single and all alone, and I had no idea how I would be able to rebuild my life.

But somehow, deep down inside, I intuitively knew that I could rebuild my life, and I would be able to transform myself to become the man I knew I wanted to become.

From that moment on, I stopped reading books on getting rich and making money, and I started reading books on personal growth and development, psychology, philosophy, metaphysics, and spirituality. I began asking myself the deeper existential questions about life, like, who am I, and why am I here, and I became committed to answering those deeper questions for myself. During this journey, I have read hundreds of books, I have spent hundreds of hours doing workshops and personal growth seminars, I have listened to countless hours of audio programs, and I've lost track of the thousands of dollars I've spent over the past 25 years or so. Has it been worth it? Absolutely, unequivocally YES!

That is how my transformation journey began, and I am still on that journey today, more than 30 years later. Fortunately, my journey has allowed me to rebuild my life, and just as I envisioned it, it has become extraordinary.

Throughout this book, I will be sharing lessons and insights that I've gained over the past 30 years, which have allowed me to build the life of my dreams. If you are reading this book, I am convinced you can do the same.

Try and imagine that you're having a conversation with a dear friend, and he is sharing some tips and strategies to support you in building the life you were born to live. He is committed to challenging you and empowering you to become the best version of yourself, and although you may get a little uncomfortable, you will trust his guidance because you trust him and believe in him. Therefore, you will follow his lead, take his advice, and apply the things he shares with you.

Are you willing to do that?

Well, let's get started!

I'd like to begin by sharing something I wrote when I was just beginning my transformational journey. During that time, I went to therapy and began journaling to deal with my depression. My therapist instructed me to write in my journal and share how I felt. At the time, I had difficulty putting my feelings into words, so I wrote this in my journal to share how I was feeling.

## The Rollercoaster

I had heard a lot about the rollercoaster. Initially, I didn't want to go and see it, but everyone kept saying, you have to check it out and get on it. It will be so much fun.

## Chapter 1: Do Not Embrace A Midlife Crisis

Reluctantly, I went to see it. It was intriguing and enticing, and it looked like fun.

You have to get on it, everyone said.

I'm not sure that I want to.

But everyone loves getting on the Rollercoaster, they said.

I don't think I'll like it.

Go ahead and try it; you'll like it, everyone said.

So, I tried it.

In the beginning, it was fun. Going round and round and up and down with friends who also seemed to be having fun was initially enjoyable.

But after a short while, I got bored and tired. I didn't want to ride it anymore. I decided that I wanted to get off.

You can't get off, everyone said.

But I'm ready to.

No one gets off the rollercoaster once they get on.

Why not?

They just don't.

But I'm ready to get off.

Why not ride it a little longer and see if you'll change your mind? they said.

Okay, I'll try it a little longer. Round and round, up and down, I went pretending that I was enjoying myself.

But after a while, I began to get angry. I was tired of the rollercoaster, and I realized that I shouldn't have gotten on it in the first place. I wanted to get off, but I didn't know how.

I'm really sick of this rollercoaster. I want to get off right now.

We're sorry, but you must stay on the rollercoaster. That's the rule.

Well, I guess I'm going to have to break the rule because I'm about to get off.

But if you break the rule, no one will like you and you will probably get hurt, they said.

I don't care about anyone else. I want to get off now. Who can I talk to about getting off this thing?

No one knows how to get off, they said.

I'm sure someone knows; I just have to find them.

It's been said that only a few people have ever gotten off this rollercoaster. And no one really knows what happened to them. Some believe that people have even been killed trying to get off. Why take that risk?

At this point, I'm willing to take that risk. I don't care what people think or what people are going to say. I refuse to keep going round and round and getting nowhere on this thing, and I must do something to get off.

I didn't know what to do, but I knew that I couldn't stay on the rollercoaster. I needed a plan, and I needed it soon. I felt like I was dying and wanted to live again.

But what about the risk? What if what they say is true? What if I really can't get off, or get killed trying to get off?

At this point, I decide that I have only one choice. And that choice is to live. I don't know what will happen, but I know if I stay on this thing, I'm already dead. I have to trust my inner instincts, take the chance, and simply jump off. I'm not sure where I'll land or if I'll get hurt or even die, but I just know that I have to jump.

So despite what everyone else was saying and the fear and uncertainty I felt, I took a deep breath and jumped. As my body was hurled through the air uncontrollably, surprisingly, I felt a deep sense of calm and inner peace, and then I did exactly what I intuitively knew I could do - I flew!

So, can you relate to the story? Have you ever felt as if you were trapped on a rollercoaster and couldn't get off? Let's break down the story and better understand how human conditioning and programming work.

At the beginning of the story, I was paying more attention to what other people were saying instead of trusting my own instincts about the rollercoaster. Like too many people, we get tangled up in peer pressure and pay more attention to what others think and say than listening to our own inner voices. When I decided to get off, I was initially more concerned with what other people would say and think, and that's why I stayed on the rollercoaster longer than I really wanted to.

It wasn't until I got bored and angry that I began to gain the courage to go against what everyone else was doing and saying. Once the boredom and pain became too great, I made a simple choice. I let go of my need to meet other people's approval and trust my gut to do what was right for me. At that point, I was willing to accept the consequences of my choices, and I trusted my own heart to make the choice to jump. Fear of jumping into the great unknown keeps most people trapped in lives of mediocrity and discontent.

The driving factor is fear. We are afraid of the unknown and uncertainty, and for some people, it feels safer to just stay on the rollercoaster and do what everyone else is doing. By trusting my inner wisdom and letting go of the need to meet other people's approval, I embraced my fears and moved through them. Once I did this, I experienced true internal freedom, which allowed me to fly away and become the man I knew I could be.

This poem expresses how I felt during the darkest period of my life. I felt trapped on a rollercoaster, and I simply wanted to get off. Gaining the courage to go to therapy was my way of jumping off the rollercoaster. It was terrifying initially, but ultimately, I learned how to fly.

Have you ever felt that way?

This poem serves as the perfect metaphor for society. Most people are trapped on the rollercoaster and have no idea how to get off. As a matter of fact, I think most people don't want to get off because it's comfortable, and most people do not like being uncomfortable. If you're reading these words right now, I will assume you are one of the courageous ones who are willing to jump and be uncomfortable, so let's jump off and dive right in and get you off the rollercoaster.

A midlife crisis is your Soul's way of saying you need to jump off the societal rollercoaster. It is an intuitive knowing that you aren't happy and content with where you are, and you are willing to leap to get from where you are to where you want to be.

As I reflect on my life, I can clearly see how I was trapped on the societal rollercoaster. I was doing everything society said I was supposed to do to be happy, but I was miserable. In retrospect, I see how being trapped on the rollercoaster caused me to make wrong choices.

First of all, I believed that having money and material things would make me happy, so I worked hard and climbed the corporate ladder, and at the age of twenty-three, I had made it by society's standards. I had a nice house, some money in the bank, an excellent credit rating, and I was able to take nice vacations. Next, I got married for all the wrong reasons. I got married believing it would make me appear more mature and help me climb the corporate ladder faster. I honestly never asked myself if my first wife was really the person I wanted to spend the rest of my life with. At twenty-one, I was too emotionally immature to even ask myself that question.

Most importantly, I realized that one of the things that drove me to become successful was my need for approval from others. Because I struggled with low self-esteem, becoming successful was a way for me to feel good about myself. This is the primary reason I sank into a deep depression after my divorce. I felt like a complete failure which compounded my feelings of low self-esteem.

These choices were the result of me being trapped on the rollercoaster.

To fully understand how we get trapped in a midlife crisis, I'd like to share another metaphor with you. The metaphor is called The Drift.

The drift is a metaphor for society. Most people float along with this societal current of conformity and aren't even conscious of it. The Drift tells us that if we make a certain amount of money, we will be happy. If we have a particular position within a large corporation, we're successful. If we get married, buy a house, have 2.5 kids (where in the hell did they get that from?) and a dog, then we are "Living the American Dream." So ultimately, we buy into this. But the truth is, we've given up our dream and fallen victim to the Drift's dream. I have to admit no one was guiltier about this than me.

As mentioned, I was floating along the drift, doing everything it said to be successful. I was floating aimlessly along with that societal current, thinking that there was only one direction to go.

The truth is, once we accomplish the Drift's dream, we rationalize it by saying we're successful. Now we no longer need to dream because we've made it. So, all we have to do now is sit back and wait for that societal safety-valve called "retirement." In a way, society tricks us into giving up our dreams. What a shame!

This is the source of a midlife crisis. When we buy into the Drift's dream and give up on our dreams, we will always feel that something is missing in our lives. We will never be fulfilled, and our lives won't have any true meaning or purpose. This feeling of emptiness is what drives a midlife crisis.

So let's set up a scenario. Imagine you're floating along the Drift. As you're floating along, something keeps pulling at you. A part of you says maybe you really don't want to be going in this direction. But then you look at everybody else and decide that you may as well continue since everybody else is. But there is something that keeps pulling at you; you ignore it. Then all of a sudden, you get stuck in the drift. Something within this current grabs you and won't let go. You keep fighting, but it's got a firm hold on you.

Now the reason most people don't get out of the Drift is that it's uncomfortable. Not only that, we're afraid of what people will say about us. So why go against the flow? But now and then, someone decides that they really don't want to go in the same direction as everybody else. They decide to stop. So what happens? People have to go around the obstruction, and they get angry and fuss and raise all sorts of hell. They try to force that person back into the flow. And usually, it works because we really don't want to cause too much trouble. Right? But if you choose to trust that still small voice within you, then you shouldn't worry about what other people think. Of course, this is easier said than done.

Let's get back to you floating down the Drift. This thing that keeps pulling on you is simply The Universe trying to remind you of your dream. It is doing everything in its power to get your attention, but you continually ignore it. So it decides that it needs to take more drastic measures because it has something for you to do, and only you can do it.

Then it sends you what I label as a "Wake-Up Call." In most cases, a wake-up call isn't a very pleasant experience. But it's usually the only way it can get your attention. I believe that we always have the opportunity to minimize the discomfort if we simply decide to listen.

My wake-up call was my divorce. For the first time in my life, I had to really look at myself at a very deep level. I was caught in the Drift, and The Universe kept telling me to grab the rope, but I wouldn't listen. As I look back, I realize I heard it. I simply chose not to listen, and it brought me an incredible amount of pain. But it knew its plan for me, and it refused to let me drift aimlessly along with the current. When I finally went on my transformational journey, I realized how I had created a lot of unnecessary pain in my life. But as soon as I started listening to and following my inner wisdom, my whole life started to make sense.

As I look back, I can definitely see the perfection in my life's journey. I have come to know that everything that comes into our lives, no matter how painful or difficult, actually brings us a gift and a lesson if we are willing to look deeply enough. If I had to do my life all over again, I wouldn't change a thing because though it was difficult, I now see how every adversity and challenge I overcame actually molded me into the man I was supposed to become. There is perfection in the Universe, and when we learn to align ourselves with that perfection, our lives become extraordinary.

In order to create an extraordinary life, do not fall victim to a midlife crisis. Make a commitment to yourself that you will go on your own transformational journey. Rest assured that you already have everything you need inside of you to begin your journey, and know that there is an inner wisdom and guidance system in you that will guide you along the way.

Be willing to jump off the rollercoaster and get out of the Drift so that you can live the life of your dreams because you deserve to be happy and fulfilled, and this book is written to be the roadmap to your true freedom.

In the next chapter, we will be talking about specific ways for you to get out of the drift and jump off the rollercoaster, so buckle up and let's get started.

I'd like to close this chapter with a few reasons for optimism about getting older. Just remember, age is just a number, and you get to choose whether or not you age gracefully. Here are a few facts from the New England Journal of Medicine.

An extensive study in the USA found that the most productive age in human life is between 60-70 years of age. The 2$^{nd}$ most productive stage of human beings is 70-80 years of age. The 3$^{rd}$ most productive stage is 50-60 years of age.

And did you know the average age of Nobel Prize winners is 62 years old? The average age of presidents of prominent companies globally is 63 years. The average age of pastors of the 100 largest churches in the US is 71, and the average age of the Popes is 76 years.

This tells us that it has been determined that the best years of your life are between 60 and 80 years. The report concluded that at age 60, you reach the top of your potential, and this continues into your 80s. Therefore, if you are between 60-70 or 70-80, you are in the Best and 2$^{nd}$ level of your life.

If you're less than 60, this should definitely give you something to look forward to. So, remember our mantra, I'm Not Okay With Gray, and go out there and build the life of your dreams.

It's never too late!

# CHAPTER 2
## Embrace Who You Are

THE KEY TO getting off of the rollercoaster and out of the drift is to awaken to who you really are. To do this, you must be willing to go on your own transformation journey. Take a moment and think about this quote from philosopher Alan Watts. "Waking up to who you are requires letting go of who you imagine yourself to be." I define transformation as the process through which we transform from who we thought we were to who we were born to be.

So who do you think you are?

There are an infinite amount of teachers, coaches, gurus, and thought leaders available to support you in waking up to who you truly are, but ultimately, it all depends on you. You have to decide for yourself that you are willing to do whatever it takes to discover who you really are and then find a teacher you trust to help you along your journey. Since you're reading this book, think of me as that trusted teacher.

As I've mentioned before, I have been on an amazing transformational journey for more than twenty-five years, yet I'm still learning and growing. I like to think of life as a life-long process of growth and transformation. Put another way, life is about evolution. We should be committed to evolving our entire lives. Evolution has no end; it is an ongoing process that continues for eternity.

Personal growth and transformation should be a wonderful journey without a finite destination. There will always be room for more growth and transformation, and your goal is to commit to the process of growth

To continue my evolution, I often ask myself one simple question. How can I become better? How can I become a better husband, a better father, a better writer, a better speaker, or a better human being? By continually asking myself this question, I am challenged to stay committed to my evolution.

As I reflect on the past 25 years of my journey, I believe that the most important lesson I have learned along the way is the importance of making peace with your past.

Over the years, I have attended motivational seminars (including walking on 1200 degree hot coals), I've been to therapy, I've learned how to meditate, I've immersed myself in sensory deprivation tanks, and I've had transcendent spiritual experiences that have connected me to a power greater than myself. But if I had to choose one thing that had the most profound impact on my life, it would have to be learning how to make peace with my past.

To add some context, I have to admit that I possibly had the worst childhood a person could have. Between the ages of six and thirteen, I experienced every imaginable type of abuse you could think of. It wasn't until I went to therapy that I learned how my traumatic childhood was negatively impacting my life as an adult.

Amazingly, some people do not believe that their childhood can actually have an adverse effect on their adult lives. Have you ever heard someone say that their parents used to beat them when they were little, yet they still turned out okay? This statement is a defense mechanism that keeps people trapped in their pain, and they will rationalize that their traumatic childhoods had no effect on them whatsoever. The truth is, if you remember being beaten as a child and you have not done any healing work, I can assure you that it will affect your life today.

I recently ran across a quote by author and spiritual teacher Iyanla Vanzant that fully embodies why making peace with your past is so important. This powerful quote holds the key to your happiness, and I suggest that you read it slowly (and several times) and intently to fully grasp the implications of its message.

*"Until you heal the wounds of your past, you are going to bleed. You can bandage the bleeding with food, with alcohol, with drugs, with work, with cigarettes, with sex; but eventually, it will all ooze through and stain your life. You must find the strength to open the wounds, stick your hands inside, pull out the core of the pain that is holding you in your past, the memories, and make peace with them."*

Herein lies the key to your happiness. Over the last twenty-plus years, I have learned that we must be willing to heal our hearts and make peace with our past if we truly want to be happy. We can read all the self-help books in the world and listen to audio programs or go to seminars with motivational speakers. Still, if we fail to carry out our healing work, we will unconsciously sabotage our lives and ultimately keep ourselves from being completely happy.

The key to making peace with your past lies in your willingness to heal any emotional scars you may carry from your childhood. Healing your heart is the key to making peace with your past. Psychologists will tell you that all addictions have an unresolved emotional conflict at their core, which simply means that there are emotional wounds that need to be healed.

What Iyanla Vanzant meant when she said, *"You must find the strength to open the wounds, stick your hands inside, pull out the core of the pain that is holding you in your past, the memories, and make peace with them"* is that it is your responsibility to look within your own heart and find where the pain is and be willing to heal that pain.

Some people prescribe to the idea that you do not have to address your childhood wounds to be successful and happy. They believe that digging up old hurts does not do any good. I completely disagree with this way of thinking. I believe that it is absolutely imperative that you look at the dark events in your life and are willing to shed light on them. Those dark places will eventually sabotage your happiness if you are unwilling to do so.

There is a term called "spiritual bypassing," which means a person refuses to heal their inner wounds because they have accepted a specific religious teaching that says that God can heal you. I used to hold that belief. At one time, I thought that if I prayed enough and followed religious dogma and doctrine, I would eventually become happy. My own experience has taught me otherwise. It wasn't until I became courageous enough to make peace with my past and deal with some childhood trauma that I was able to heal my heart and become genuinely happy.

When I decided that I wanted to heal my wounds, I was introduced to a man named John Bradshaw, who facilitated a program called Healing Your Inner Child. In one of his workshops, I learned how my abusive childhood was at the core of all the dysfunction in my life. I learned that I had abandonment issues as a result of being separated from my mom when I was six years old, and I also learned that for the majority of my adult life, I was driven by a deep sense of shame. It was my internal feelings of shame that drove me to be successful. I worked really hard to gain other people's approval because I didn't feel worthy.

Although it was extremely difficult, I made a choice to heal my heart and make peace with my past. I took Iyanla's advice and found the strength to open my wounds, stick my hands inside, and pull out the core of my pain that kept me trapped in my past - and I made peace with them.

As a result of doing this work, I can honestly admit that I am happiest now than I've ever been in my life in this very moment. It definitely wasn't easy, but I can assure you that it was worth it.

I hope you will take some time and really think about what I've shared. Do not make the same mistakes that I did in thinking that being positive all the time will solve all of your problems. Of course, there is absolutely nothing wrong with being positive, and I am still a huge advocate of positive thinking. The key is to make sure that you aren't hiding behind positivity because of some unresolved emotional pain the way I did.

If you are committed to making peace with your past and are looking for some ways to do so, let me make a few suggestions for you to consider. First of all, it's imperative for you to be willing to seek support if needed. I realize that there is a lot of negative stigmas attached to seeking support, but seeking support is a sign of strength, not weakness.

Here are a few things to consider if you are truly ready to make peace with your past.

First of all, there is nothing wrong with seeking out a good therapist to support you in dealing with any emotional challenges you may be facing. Our society has conditioned us to believe that we are supposed to carry the world's weight on our shoulders and not seek support, but this simply isn't true. We all need support at one time or another, so if you've been looking for ways to help you make peace with your past, a good therapist may be exactly what you need.

I would like to share an article I wrote a while ago that shares my first experience with therapy. I hope that it will give you some insight into how difficult and challenging it might be and inspire you to take the first step if you think you will benefit from therapy.

The article is titled Men's Emotional Healing.

In 1989, I had a series of traumatic experiences that were beginning to take their toll. My divorce and separation from my kids were extremely painful and negatively impacted my life. I had slipped into a deep state of depression and was barely able to function daily. As my depression deepened, I went into isolation, where I literally shut myself off from the outside world.

Although I could go to work and function in that capacity, I was completely disconnected from any social settings. I was not dating, and I did not socialize with my friends. I also had difficulty sleeping. I would rarely eat and had begun to lose weight, which was rare for me, being a former personal trainer who took excellent care of my physical body. After several months, I began to have fleeting thoughts of suicide, and it appeared that my situation was hopeless. To alleviate some of the pain, I began to read books dealing with depression.

As I read them, I could see myself in some of the stories. I definitely had all of the symptoms of depression, and I knew that I had to deal with it head-on if I ever wanted to get my life back on track. After reading several books, I realized that I was still deeply depressed and had not really begun to deal with the issues that were causing my depression. Instinctively I knew that I needed help, and I decided to seek therapy.

After deciding to get help, another series of challenges surfaced. First of all, how was I going to find a therapist? How would I know which one to choose? What if the therapist couldn't help me? Would I be able to change? Could therapy fix me? What about the money to pay for it? I was completely broke and could not afford to pay someone to listen to my problems. What was I going to do? These were just a few of the questions going through my mind.

My greatest fear was wondering what would happen if my employees found out. As a manager, I was considered the leader, and I definitely did not want to appear weak in front of my co-workers. I believed that I needed to keep this a secret so that I would not lose the respect of my employees. In addition, I did not want my superiors to know because I thought I might lose my job if they found out.

After a few months of agonizing over these questions, I knew that I had to take the chance and try therapy. I didn't have any other choice. It was seek help or die - there was no gray area. I decided that I definitely wanted to live, and I somehow gained the courage to seek out a therapist.

My first attempt at therapy did not go well. I walked into the therapist's office and pretended that I was seeking information for a friend. I'm sure the people there knew this was a lie, but they allowed me to walk out with some of their brochures and a phone number to their suicide hotline.

To be honest, I was absolutely terrified. But although I was scared, deep down, I knew that I would have to gain the courage to try again. I waited a few days and tried a different therapist's office. This time I had a completely different result.

As I walked into the office, I believe the receptionist picked up on my fear. I began asking her questions about depression and whether or not they had any books that I could read. All of a sudden, a therapist walked out and began asking me questions. "May I help you?" she asked. "Not really. I'm just looking for some information about depression." "Are you depressed?" "I'm not really sure," I answered. "Why don't you come into my office so we can talk a little. Is that alright?"

"I guess so."

As I followed her into her office, it felt as if my heart would jump out of my chest. I was so nervous and afraid that I was dripping with sweat. She obviously picked up on this and began to put my mind at ease.

"What is your name?"

"Michael."

"Well, Michael, I can sense that you are a little nervous, so let me start by asking what I can do to help you. Is there anything I can do for you?"

"Well, maybe. I have been doing some research about depression, and I think I'm depressed, but I'm really not sure."

"Do you feel depressed?"

"Based on what I've read so far, I think I am. But to be completely honest, I'm not sure I know exactly what depression is supposed to feel like. Does that make any sense to you?"

"It makes a lot of sense to me. Unfortunately, most men do not recognize how they feel. Men have been conditioned to disconnect from their emotions, which makes it extremely difficult for them to express how they really feel. Most men will tell you what they think, but they usually do not know how they feel. You apparently fit into this category."

"I'm not sure if I really understand what you are saying, but a part of me thinks you are right."

"You just validated the point I made. You are currently speaking from an intellectual perspective instead of an emotional one. It sounds as if you are disconnected from your emotions."

"Let's assume you are right. If I am disconnected from my emotions, how do I get reconnected? Do you have any books on how to do this?"

"Unfortunately, you cannot reconnect to your emotions by reading books. For you to reconnect, you have to relearn how to feel. This can be accomplished through therapy with me or any trained therapist."

"I really don't understand what you mean. But if I decide to relearn how to feel, how long will it take?"

"I really can't answer that question. It's really up to you and how committed you are to doing the work."

"What do you mean doing the work? What kind of work is involved?"

"In the therapeutic community, we use the word 'work' because it takes a considerable amount of effort to heal yourself so that you can reconnect with your emotions. Doing the work means that you become willing to open yourself up on an emotional level. This can be quite difficult at times."

"Well, I believe I'm ready. I'm really tired of being alone, and I definitely want to experience some fun in my life again. I think I can do this, so how much will it cost?"

"I operate on a sliding scale based on your ability to pay. The most important thing is for you to make the commitment to yourself to heal, and we can address the money issue at a later date. Are you ready to begin? Let's set up a date and time for you to begin your healing."

"I just wanted to thank you for being so nice and understanding. The truth is, I was about to run out of your office before you showed up. Now I'm really glad I came because I believe that you can help me."

"That is a great attitude to have. I'm glad that you trust me enough to work with you. Just remember that I can guide you, but you must be willing to do the work. As long as you believe that you can heal, I assure you that you will. Just stay committed and trust the process, and you will be just fine. The truth is, you have already done the hard part by showing up today. It takes an incredible amount of courage to be here, and I'm really proud of you for taking the first step."

As I left the therapist's office that day, I knew I had just taken the biggest step of my life. I didn't know what to expect, but I knew I was willing to do whatever it took to heal my emotions and relearn how to feel. I became committed to my own healing, and I can now say that I am emotionally healed and connected to my authentic self.

As the therapist mentioned, it wasn't easy, but it was definitely possible. It has been one of the most challenging yet most fulfilling journeys of my life.

I cannot put into words the joy I feel regularly as a result of doing my emotional work. My relationships now work, my creativity and sense of reverence are enhanced, my love of nature has been rekindled, and my professional life is rewarding and fulfilling. I took the road less traveled, and it has made all the difference in the world for me.

I wanted to share this story because there is such a negative stigma about men and therapy that I believe it's time for a new conversation. In this new conversation, men will recognize the importance of healing their emotions and put forth the effort to do their healing work.

When we learn to support each other in our growth, we can remove the fear and stigma of being emotionally vulnerable, which will ultimately result in us being happier human beings. I personally believe that this is the most important work men can participate in, and we must begin supporting each other through this process.

If we gain the courage to do this work, we will see a decline in domestic violence, child abuse, alcoholism, and random acts of violence. The time has come for a new conversation about our emotional healing.

Are you willing to join the conversation?

So the first step in making peace with your past is to be willing to do your emotional work. You can do this with a therapist, a life coach, through workshops, and even online seminars.

Once you do your inner work, it's important to have a support network of like-minded people who are willing to support you and hold you accountable for continuing your growth and healing. And once you've made peace with your past, it's time to start asking yourself deeper questions about what it means to be a human being.

So let's begin with this question, "Who are you?"

If you ask most people who they are, they will usually respond with answers such as their name, whether they have a family, what they do for a living, if they are a democrat or republican, an African American or Caucasian, a Christian or a Muslim (or are part of a host of other religions), an American or Asian - the list of labels goes on and on. But if you think really deeply about this, these are just titles and labels that we use to try to define who we are. To prove my point, I want you to do a simple test. Walk up to a mirror and ask yourself what you see. Do you see a republican? A Christian? A husband? A manager?

The answer is that you see a human being. The mirror will only reflect that which is placed in front of it. All the titles and labels that you use to define yourself are simply titles, labels, and beliefs that you have accepted as who and what you are. For example, have you ever known someone who used to be a republican but then became a democrat? Or someone who was a Christian, who then became a Muslim? Or maybe someone who was pro-life then became pro-choice? If they looked in the mirror as a republican and then became a democrat, what would they see in the mirror? They would see a human being, not a label. Labels are really just beliefs. You are not a label. You are a human being with different beliefs, and although your beliefs may change, you will not.

What you see in the mirror is what you truly are, but it goes deeper than that.

*What* you are, is not necessarily *who* you are.

Let me explain in more detail.

*What* you are is a human being with flesh and bones. This is an undisputable fact. But *who* you are is the divine being that resides within the flesh and bones. Here is another way to look at it - if I stand in front of a mirror and look at myself wearing a shirt, I will say, this is my shirt, so who owns it? I do - it is my shirt. Now, I continue to look into the mirror and notice my body. Who is the *me* that owns the body? If this is my body, who am I? I would like to suggest that the me that owns the body is actually my spirit. Put another way, you are not actually a human being having a spiritual experience - you are a spiritual being having a human experience, and your body is just like a suit of clothes you are wearing.

So what do you think? Do you believe this? Can you accept that you are much more than your physical body? Can you embrace the idea that you are a divine spiritual being with unlimited potential who has the capacity to be, do, or have anything your heart desires?

If you are willing to embrace this idea, then you have the keys to ensure that you never experience a midlife crisis. The cure for a midlife crisis is to know who and what you are as a spiritual being.

You are actually a three-part being which can be described as body, mind, and spirit. You are a spirit, which is housed in a body that has a mind. Your body is like the clothes you are wearing, and your mind is like a tool that you use to help make conscious decisions and learn new things. They all work in harmony.

As a spiritual being, you have an infinite capacity for learning and creativity. There are absolutely no limits to the number of things you can learn and create. You are only limited by your imagination, and even your imagination is unlimited.

So, let's break down the three parts of your being.

Let's begin with your mind.

It's important that you understand what your mind is and how it works if you truly want to discover who you really are. Your mind and your brain are not necessarily the same thing. Your brain is the organ that serves as the center of your nervous system and is responsible for cognitive thinking and memory. In my opinion, it is the most amazing organ in your body, and it works just like a muscle - the more you use it, the stronger it gets.

The mind, however, is separate and distinct from the brain, although they work together. It is almost impossible to truly define the mind. Scientists have been trying to define it in scientific terms for millennia, but unfortunately, there has never been a consensus on exactly what the mind is. Rather than try to argue and define it, I will simply share a definition that I truly resonate with, and it is this definition I will use to explain what I believe the mind does and how it works.

The mind is *the element of a person that enables them to be aware of the world and their experiences, to think, and to feel; the faculty of consciousness and thought.*

I really like the last part of this definition; *the faculty of consciousness and thought.*

According to Dr. Bruce Lipton, author of the amazing book The Biology Of Belief, the mind actually has two parts; the conscious mind and the subconscious mind. A great metaphor to explain how it works is the iceberg. If you look at an iceberg in the ocean, you will only see a small portion of it above the water, but did you know that in some cases, 90% of the iceberg is actually below the surface? This is how the mind works. The top 10% is your conscious mind, and the lower 90% is your subconscious mind. What is really fascinating is that the subconscious mind is 1000 times more powerful than the conscious mind when it comes to influencing your behavior.

Dr. Lipton explained it this way:

*When we are born, we are completely conscious of all the external stimuli that we interact with. As children, we process primarily through our feelings without judgment or thought about the situation. In other words, we use our hearts, not our minds, to interpret everything around us. Our feelings become the guidepost of our experiences.*

*During the first 7-10 years of our lives, our subconscious mind works like a video recorder. It simply records all the external events in our lives, and then it begins associating feelings, memories, and beliefs with those events. As we grow older, we begin to form subconscious beliefs about everything we come into contact with. As we form these beliefs, we then begin making assumptions about who we are and how we fit into the world. Our prerecorded tapes become our subconscious beliefs about ourselves, and everything we think and do is then filtered through, and influenced by these prerecorded tapes.*

So take a moment to think about your own childhood, especially between when you were born and when you turned seven. What do you remember? Do you remember growing up in a loving, caring home, or was it filled with violence and dysfunction?

Whether you realize it or not, your childhood strongly impacts your behavior, even as an adult. If you remember being loved and nurtured as a child, the chances are your subconscious mind is filled with positive beliefs about yourself. In other words, your prerecorded tapes are positive, which in most cases means you will feel good about yourself and have a positive attitude about life. On the other hand, if you remember pain and misery growing up, there is a good chance that your prerecorded tapes about yourself may be negative, which in turn may cause you to create a negative outlook on life.

You can look at the subconscious mind as a big memory bank that stores your beliefs, memories, and life experiences. All your thoughts are instantly processed through your subconscious beliefs. Look at it this way - once your subconscious tapes are programmed during your childhood, every thought and action you have as an adult will be based on the programming you experienced growing up.

Here is an example from my own life.

I was separated from my mom at the age of six, where I then created a subconscious belief that the people who love you will always leave you. As an adult, that may sound irrational, but as a six-year-old, my mother meant the world to me and having her leave me was devastating and emotionally traumatizing.

As a result of this event, I created a subconscious belief that there was something wrong with me that caused my mother to leave. The primary belief I created was that I was unlovable. In order not to feel the shame and abandonment I experienced when my mother left, I created an unconscious strategy that I thought would keep me from feeling pain and keep people in my life from leaving.

That strategy was for me to become a super nice guy in hopes of keeping people around that I cared about. By becoming a super nice guy, I put other people's emotional and psychological needs ahead of my own. I was constantly trying to take care of others before taking care of myself. This is called *co-dependence*, and it was the reason I struggled with relationships earlier in my life.

I didn't realize this as I was growing up, but that single event laid the foundation for how I interacted in all of my relationships as an adult. My subconscious beliefs about myself sabotaged my relationships.

I would enter into a relationship where I would be the super nice guy. I would do all the right things that a woman would want in a relationship. I was attentive and respectful, and I had no problems showing affection. I had a great sense of humor and definitely believed in monogamy. On the surface, I appeared to be the perfect guy, but unfortunately, my subconscious beliefs about not being good enough and the deep-seated fear of abandonment kept me from being truly authentic in relationships, which kept me from experiencing true intimacy. No matter how much a woman loved me, that deep-rooted fear I had convinced me that something was wrong with me, which led to the fear that eventually, the women in my life would leave.

Based on this subconscious fear, what do you think happened in my relationships? Of course, the women in my life would leave. I created an amazing pattern in my relationships, especially after my divorce. I would enter into a relationship, and it would last two to three weeks, and then the women would end up saying that they cared too much about me to stay in the relationship.

At the time, it made absolutely no sense to me that women would say that. How could you care about someone but at the same time leave them? After some deep self-introspection and emotional healing, I recognized how my subconscious beliefs had been sabotaging my relationships, and I figured out how to break the pattern.

The point I'm trying to make is how powerful the subconscious mind really is. Remember, the subconscious mind is separate and distinct from your brain - it is the faculty of consciousness and thought.

On the other hand, you have your conscious mind, which could be referred to as your intellect. The conscious mind is where you store information that you have learned through rigorous study and learning. When you go to school and learn facts, you use your conscious mind.

When you calculate and figure out solutions to most problems, you are also using your conscious mind, but remember what I said about the subconscious mind being 1000 times more powerful than the conscious mind?

Here is an example of how this works.

Imagine that you know someone that has a PhD in astrophysics. This person is obviously brilliant, and has a highly-developed conscious mind. But imagine too that this person has difficulty creating healthy relationships. No matter what they do, they always experience difficulty in relationships. Why do you think this is? They are very smart, yet they can't create fulfilling relationships.

Why is that?

Well, it's actually pretty simple. On a conscious level, they can read a book about relationships and explain to you intellectually how relationships work, which uses the conscious mind. But their subconscious is 1000 times more powerful than their conscious mind, so when they enter into a relationship, the subconscious beliefs they have about themselves will always override the conscious mind. No matter how many books they read or how smart they are, if they have deeply rooted negative subconscious beliefs about themselves, they will never be able to create healthy relationships.

This is why it is so important to understand how the mind works. No matter how much we may learn on a conscious level, we can never truly change our lives if we aren't willing to look at our subconscious beliefs. We each have deeply held subconscious beliefs about a wide variety of things, and until we become willing to change these subconscious beliefs, we will not be able to overcome our subconscious conditioning.

Lets take a look at some subconscious beliefs that may be sabotaging your life right now.

Are you currently struggling financially and can't figure out why? There is a very good chance that your subconscious beliefs are keeping you from being financially secure. If you grew up hearing that money was the root of all evil or that rich people were stuck up and selfish, you may have subconscious beliefs that keep you from making a lot of money because your subconscious belief might be that money is bad.

If you're a man and you struggle with relationships, you may have subconscious beliefs that women only want you for your money or can't be trusted. This belief will eventually sabotage any new relationship you enter. If you're a woman and struggle with relationships, then it's quite possible that you have subconscious beliefs that say all men are dogs and only want sex. Therefore, this belief will keep you from creating true intimacy with men because of your lack of trust. If you happen to be religious, you may have subconscious beliefs that you are a sinner, and there is nothing you can do except repent of your sins and hope that God forgives you for being a sinner.

No matter what subconscious beliefs you have, you must understand that those subconscious beliefs are actually the cause of most of the pain, suffering, and lack of experience you have in life. To sum it up, your subconscious beliefs create your reality, so if you aren't happy with any area of your life right now, I can assure you that the main reason is that you have some unconscious belief that is causing you pain and misery.

It is imperative that you begin examining your deeply held subconscious beliefs if you truly want to change, but rest assured that it is possible to do so.

Now that you have a deeper understanding of how the subconscious mind works, the really good news - when you realize just how powerful the mind is, you can use it to create anything you want in life.

Have you ever heard this quote: Whatever the mind can conceive, you can achieve, if you really believe?

## Do you believe it? Is it really possible?

I believe the answer is yes, and now I would like to share how and why this is possible. So let's go back to the definition I posted earlier: The mind is *the element of a person that enables them to be aware of the world and their experiences, to think, and to feel; the faculty of consciousness and thought.*

I would like you to focus on *the faculty of consciousness and thought.*

Here is another way to look at it. Try to imagine there is a Divine Intelligence that permeates the Universe. This Intelligence is actually the Source of all things. It is inherent in all things. It is what keeps the planets aligned and causes a seed to grow into a flower. The same intelligence causes a bone to heal and the earth to orbit the sun.

There are many different names for this Source, but the name does not matter. You can call it God, The Creator, Yahweh, Jehovah, Great Spirit, The Universe, or any other name, but what is most important is that you believe and trust that it is available to you (throughout this book, I will refer to it as The Source, Divine Intelligence, The Universe, and God). You do not have to believe in any particular religion or dogma to have access to it. You must simply open your heart and mind to the truth that it exists. If you accept this truth, you must accept that your mind is connected to The Source. Your mind is like a conduit through which The Source allows divine intelligence to flow to you and through you.

Now you must remember what I said at the beginning. **The mind and the brain are not the same thing.** The brain can only process information that you have provided to it. The brain is not creative - it is not the source of imagination, creativity, or divine ideas. The brain is also not the source of inspiration or insight; these are all functions of the mind, which can also be referred to as the heart, or the center of your being.

Author and spiritual teacher Iyanla Vanzant said *The mind is a powerful, creative energy. Everything we think, do, and feel begins in the mind. For this reason, we have perceptions that we hold in our minds.*

The quote "whatever the mind can conceive you can achieve" is true because The Source of all things is purely creative and needs you to co-create with it. So when your mind conceives a divine idea from The Source, which is all-powerful and limitless, you can accomplish it if you're willing to work hand-in-hand with The Source and put forth a lot of effort to bring it to fruition.

One of my favorite spiritual teachers is Deepak Chopra. He shared a very powerful quote that speaks to this truth. He said, "Inherent in every intention and desire are the mechanics for its fulfillment." Put another way, The Source will not give you an idea that you can't accomplish. The Source knows exactly what you're capable of and will therefore only give you divine ideas that are attainable for you. You wouldn't even have the idea in the first place if you weren't capable of accomplishing it.

As I mentioned previously, the mind is the source of imagination, and therefore it is the key to creating anything you want in life. Let me share a brief story with you to validate my point.

During the darkest period of my life, I was deeply depressed and unsure of how I would get my life back on track. At the time, I had no money, job, relationship, or material possessions, and things seemed pretty hopeless. But the one thing I did have was my imagination, and I began to use it to help me change my situation. Despite that I had absolutely nothing, I began imagining my life getting better. I focused my attention on what I did have. I would begin each day counting my blessings for everything that I had, such as my health, my ability to learn, my positive attitude, a few close friends, children who loved me, and the fact that I was even alive.

I began envisioning what my life would be like once I got back on my feet, and I somehow knew that eventually, I would. As I continued to focus on the things that I did have and on the future that I wanted to create, things slowly started to change for me. Eventually, I found a job, then I purchased a car, and finally, I was able to get my own apartment. Although this took a couple of years, my point is that I used my imagination to see the things I wanted, and then I worked really hard to get them. It all began in my mind. I had to be willing to use my mind and imagination first before I could create the things I wanted.

In retrospect, I can now see how The Source was actually the source of all of the ideas that I used to put my life back together. It was The Source that would provide me with ideas on where to look for employment, and that gave me the inspiration to remain positive even when I had nothing. The Source gave me the strength and courage to move through all of my life challenges and not fall victim to despair.

It was The Source that encouraged me and helped me to focus on my ultimate destiny, and it didn't allow me to quit.

Even through those difficult times, I held on to my dreams of one day being a successful entrepreneur, writer, and speaker. I had no evidence that I could do these things; I only had the belief and faith. Belief and faith originate in the mind, and I now recognize that each of these originates from The Source.

And now here I am, some twenty plus years later doing exactly what I imagined I would be doing. All because I chose to believe that whatever the mind can conceive, you can achieve.

You must understand I am no different than you are. I am a divine spiritual being with direct access to The Source, and so are you. You have a mind and direct access to The Source. There is nothing you cannot accomplish if you choose to access your divinity, but it is up to you to go a little deeper and figure out what negative subconscious beliefs you may have about yourself and change them. It is your responsibility to learn more about your mind and begin using it to create the life you deserve. This is simply an overview of how your mind works, but for now, I simply want you to accept and understand that your mind is the most important aspect of your humanity. Do not take it for granted. Use it to create the life you were born to live. It is your greatest gift from The Source.

So now, let's talk about your body.

I believe that the most amazing thing on this planet is the human body. I do not believe that there is anything more miraculous. Although most people take their bodies for granted, I believe it is the greatest gift that The Source provided us with. I mentioned earlier that the body is simply a suit of clothing your spirit wears, so I must admit that The Source knew exactly what it was doing when it created the human body.

Of course, everyone is aware of their own physical body, but did you know that you also have an emotional or energetic body?

If you accept that you are a spiritual being, it makes it easier to grasp how the emotional/energetic body works.

Think of it this way:

Imagine that you have an opening in the top of your skull, and there is a pipe that goes from the top of your skull to the bottom of your belly. This pipe flows with energy that comes directly from The Source; this energy is your life force, and it permeates your entire being. When you are born, the pipe is completely open, and it allows Source energy to flow through you easily. This energy causes you to feel alive and connected to life. This energy is then converted into feelings, which is the spirit's way of communicating with the body. There are primarily four energies that move throughout the energetic body; happiness, anger, sadness, and fear.

As a child, whenever you experienced one of these feelings, you acted appropriately and expressed the feeling through an emotion. For example, if you felt sad, you would cry; if you felt angry, you would scream or lash out; if you felt happy, you would smile and laugh, and if you felt fear, you would close off or retreat. As long as you expressed the feeling appropriately, then the energetic pipe stayed open and clear and your life force energy continues to flow through you.

As you grow older, your parents or family members begin conditioning you to believe that expressing them is wrong, so you begin to repress and suppress your feelings, and each time you do, you begin to create little energy blocks in the pipe. It's like building up plaque in your arteries. The more you suppress your feelings, the more the energetic pipe clogs up, and before you know it, the pipe is completely closed, and you are cut off from your life force. When this happens, you lose your sense of aliveness because the divine flow of energy has been cut off. Once the flow of energy has been cut off and we have been disconnected from The Source, we then learn to process everything through our conscious mind or intellect, and we become very rational and analytical. In other words, we try to rely on our brains instead of our minds and hearts.

The bad news is that the energetic body works like the subconscious mind. We may not be aware of it, but our repressed emotions cause us to act out irrationally sometimes because we are completely unconscious of the pain we may be carrying. Here is a good example.

Have you ever met someone or known someone who is always angry? No matter what is going on, this person is angry and negative, and they usually aren't that pleasant to be around. They get angry and upset at the slightest provocation, and no matter what you say or do, they will negatively respond to just about everything. Do you know anyone like that? Are *you* like that?

Why do you think this person acts this way?

It's because they have trapped emotional energy in their emotional body, and until they learn how to release it, they will always act out of anger.

On the flip side of that, maybe you know someone who always pretends to be happy. They are the people-pleasing types who always seek approval and pretend that everything is always okay. The only emotion they express is happiness, but unfortunately, they are completely sad and emotionally bankrupt. A person like this usually has trapped anger, fear, or sadness in their emotional bodies, and rather than feel these emotions, they hide behind being happy all of the time.

When we have repressed or suppressed emotions, they can sabotage all areas of our lives. As long as we feel and release our feelings appropriately, the life force can move through us, but as we shut down the flow, we create a disconnection from The Source, and it leads to all sorts of problems in our lives.

It's vital that you take care of your physical body and your emotional one. You take care of the physical body by eating the right foods and exercising. You take care of the emotional body by investing in some emotional healing work that allows you to release any repressed energy that is trapped in your emotional body.

Now that you have a better understanding of how the mind and the body work together, understand who you really are.

Every major religion promotes a very simple and profound truth. There is a Source through which all things are created. It does not matter which religion you follow, as long as you accept this simple fact. This Source is the Divine Intelligence that created and is still creating the Universe, and you have unlimited access to this Source. As a human being, you are a divine expression of this Source, which means that you can co-create anything your heart desires with this Source.

Think of it this way - if you look at the ocean, you will see a powerful, beautiful, and seemingly infinite body of water. If you walk up to the ocean and scoop up a small cup of it, what you will have in the cup is ocean. But the cup of ocean could never be the ocean in its totality, so it is a divine expression of the ocean. This expression is no different from the ocean; as a matter of fact, it contains all of the same qualities, characteristics, and attributes of the ocean. In fact, it is the ocean in an individualized expression. As long as the expression of the ocean stays connected to the ocean, it will thrive and express exactly the way the ocean does. But if the ocean in the cup is separated from the ocean, eventually, it will dry up and no longer exist as that unique expression.

The Source is just like the ocean. You are an individual expression of the Source. You have all the same qualities, characteristics, and attributes as the Source. You are no different from The Source. As long as you stay connected to The Source, you can co-create with it, and since The Source is infinite, so are you.

Do not buy into societal labels and constructs that will convince you that there is something wrong with you. Disregard all labels and titles and understand that you are a divine spiritual being with unlimited potential. The only thing that can keep you from accomplishing anything is yourself. This includes letting go of the attachment to your ethnic identity. You should definitely be proud of your ethnic heritage, whatever it may be, but you must understand that your spiritual nature has nothing to do with skin color or nationality. The Source transcends race, and therefore so do you if you choose to accept who and what you truly are.

Titles and labels will only hold you back, but accepting the truth of your being will definitely set you free. Remember that you are a three-part-being, Spirit, Mind, and Body - that is connected to The Source, and you can therefore co-create anything your heart desires.

Herein lies the key to avoiding a midlife crisis. Discover who and what you truly are, and figure out how to express your unique gifts and talents with the world.

When you do this, your life will become extraordinary!

*"I define spirituality as the moment-to-moment recognition and acknowledgement of my connection to a power greater than myself. I choose to call this power Divine Intelligence."*

**— Coach Michael Taylor**

# CHAPTER 3
## Embrace Spirituality

According to a Pew report, more and more people are moving away from organized religion. While some may see this as a move away from morality, I see it as a movement more toward developing an intimate connection with Divine Intelligence. I don't believe most people are moving away from believing in God. They are actually moving toward gaining a deeper understanding and connection to God. Now more than ever, people are identifying with the term "spiritual," not "religious" and I believe there is a huge distinction between the two.

As a former Atheist, I remember struggling with organized religion from a very young age. The biggest problem I had with religion was it simply didn't make any sense to me. It was illogical, and there were too many hypocrisies and inconsistencies within the religion of my youth.

What I have come to know (after going on my own twenty-five-year journey to find my truth about God) is that you can be spiritual without being religious. You do not have to adhere to any religious dogma or doctrine, and it is your responsibility to find your "truth" about God. To do so, you must be willing to challenge your deepest held beliefs and ideas about God that you may have unconsciously accepted.

To help you on your journey, I would like to share an excerpt from my book, What If Jesus Were A Coach? The book intends to provide readers with a positive approach to religion and Christianity. It is designed to help you discover your truth and to support you in finding the path that nurtures your soul and guides you to find the God of your understanding. You can learn more about the book at www.jesuswasacoach.com. It is available as a paperback, e-book and audio book, and I highly recommend that you pick up a copy. It shares my journey to finding my truth, and I'm certain it will support you in finding your own.

Here is what The Prairies Book Review (A professional book reviewer site) had to say about the book:

### Contemplative, absorbing, and insightful... Truly a wonderful book.

*"Taylor shares the spiritual pathway to connect with God without following strict religious doctrines that usually surround Christianity in his soul-searching latest book. He talks about his early childhood and later adult experiences with organized religion, his time as an atheist, his shifting views about God's existence—Jesus as a figure of fear to the one who is a friend and teacher—and his complete acceptance of the Unity Church's teachings of Christianity. Arguing that at some point, every human being must engage in their own journey, Taylor stresses on the importance of trusting your own wisdom: it's only through recognition of your own call that you can realize your divine purpose and discover the unique gifts and talents that allow you to support others in their journey as well. Dismissing the basic concepts of sin, hell, and punishment, the integral theme of organized religion in Christianity, Taylor stresses on the significance of meditation and mindfulness. He speaks of the teachings of Christianity but his teachings are devoid of religious dogma and doctrine. He makes his case logically, along the way presenting splendid evidence and arguments against the idea of a God who has all the emotions of humans and behaves and acts like a human, who is not a loving God, and who is ready to punish you when you displease him. Putting all together, he demonstrates that much we*

*have assumed about the biggest questions of God's existence is in fact man-made—and is therefore in need of reevaluation. Taylor's insights into the existence of God are well-presented and invite the reader into a place of quiet contemplation and compassion. This is a must-read for everyone, including non-believers."*

Here is another five star review the book received:

*"What If Jesus Were A Coach? is one of the most unique and authentic self-help spiritual books I've read in a long time. Coach Michael Taylor cites examples and quotes from experts in a spectrum of fields and seamlessly incorporates them with a set of well-researched guidelines to help readers forge their paths to attaining spiritual enlightenment. Taylor's work touches upon the teachings of all major religions, and he makes a compelling argument on how they all guide people toward the same goal, just through different paths. Taylor's inspiring words are rooted in science, theology, and spirituality. He even cites the teachings of prominent scientists such as Albert Einstein and Nikola Tesla to drive home his message. Highly recommended."*

*Pikasho Deka*

As is the case with this entire book, my goal is not to convince you that God is real. I intend to provide you with some insights and wisdom to help you come to your own conclusions.

Now take a moment to open your heart and mind and check out the excerpt chapter from the book.

---

Growing up as a child, I remember the picture of Jesus hanging up in my grandparents' home. It was the familiar picture of the white Jesus with a light emanating from his heart, symbolizing his love for humanity. I also remember the Jesus nailed on the cross wall hanging sculpture which also hung on their walls. Even as a child, I didn't understand why Jesus was white, and why did he hate black people so much?

You see, my grandparents were extremely religious even though they never went to church. As I mentioned in a previous chapter, they forced me to go to church, yet they never attended. This definitely caused some major conflicts in my mind because even though they talked a lot about Jesus, their actions did not reflect Jesus' teachings. My grandmother was a raging alcoholic who physically and verbally abused me. How could I follow Jesus when the grownup responsible for raising me was such a terrible person?

On the other hand, my grandfather was a quiet gentleman who was deeply religious and filled with wisdom. Even though he only had an eighth-grade education, he was one of the smartest men I've ever known. Some of my fondest memories from childhood were having conversations with him just about anything. We would sit outside in the yard amongst a myriad of farm animals, and he would share stories about a wide variety of topics, including life. Even though I was just a kid, he talked to me as though I was much older, and he challenged me to always think about things very deeply.

One day, I asked him why God was so angry at black people. This was during the civil rights movement as I watched news stories of black people being attacked by dogs, sprayed with fire hoses, and being beaten by cops. My young ten-year-old mind couldn't understand why black people were so mistreated. So in my mind, I concluded that black people must have done something really bad since Jesus didn't step in and stop the abuse black people were enduring.

When I asked the question, he picked up on the sadness and fear in my voice, and he lifted me and placed me on his knee. He then told me that God wasn't angry at black people. He said that God had a perfect plan, and even though we may not fully understand it, God's plan was perfect. But how could God's plan be so perfect while black people were being so mistreated? He told me not to worry and to trust the divine plan of God.

As a ten-year-old, I couldn't fully understand what he meant. I tried to rationalize how God's plan was perfect, but I just couldn't see

## Chapter 3: Embrace Spirituality

it. In retrospect, and as an adult now, I can definitely understand the perfection of the plan he was talking about. Still, it has taken me years of deep self-introspection and research to fully grasp the implications of what my grandfather told me.

I'm reminded of a quote by Albert Einstein that said, "If you can't explain your subject to an eighth-grader, you don't fully understand your topic." With that being said, I'd like to share how I now see God and how I came to my understanding.

First of all, I think most people see God as this anthropomorphic being that resides up in heaven somewhere. Since most people in the West are Christians, they have this common view that God is some old guy in the clouds who is taking notes of their lives and waiting for them to "sin" so he can banish them to eternal damnation in a fiery hell. This is one of the greatest erroneous filled teachings of most organized western religions. The error is thinking and believing that God is a human being just like us. Since God is just like us, he must have human emotions and needs, and therefore organized religions have built an entire theology based on the idea that God acts like a human. Why else would he create the ten commandments? Why else would we have to prove our love for him so he wouldn't punish us? Does it make sense to you that an omniscient and omnipresent God would get angry at you for making mistakes? Does it make sense to you that God is a jealous God? These things do not make sense to me, which is why I've always had an issue with organized religion.

The reason most people see God as a human being can be traced to Genesis 1:27, where it says, "So God created man in his own image, in the image of God he created him; male and female he created them." This verse has been misinterpreted, and most religions have concluded that this passage implies that God looks like a human being. But if you read John 4:24, it should clarify who and what God is. It says, "God is spirit, and his worshipers must worship in the Spirit and in truth."

As it says, "God is spirit," and since we were made in the image and after the likeness of God, that means we are spirit also.

According to Dr. Wayne Dyer (author and spiritual teacher), we are not human beings having a spiritual experience, we are spiritual beings having a human experience. If you can embrace this idea, rest assured this book will make a lot more sense.

Since most people see Jesus as the personification of God in human form, they have accepted this erroneous belief that God must think and act just like a human being. This is the origin of most conflicts in the world. Believing that God is a "who" instead of a "what." Put another way, God is more of a "something" instead of a "someone". It is my belief that God is the Divine Intelligence that created and is still creating this amazing Universe we live in. Seeing God this way answers another question I had as a child, which was "where was God before the Universe began?"

To answer that question, let's begin by listening to two of the most brilliant men and greatest minds the world has ever seen.

Albert Einstein once said, "Everything is energy, that's just the way that it is. Match the frequency of the reality you want to create and there is no way you can't create that reality. It can be no other way. This isn't philosophy, this is physics."

Nikola Tesla said, "If you want to understand the Universe, you must think in terms of energy, frequency, and vibration."

Both of these brilliant minds point to a scientific fact. Everything is energy!

So, where did this energy come from? This is the million-dollar question!

To answer it, you have three options.

Option 1. It was a random act that just happened.

Option 2. Something caused it to happen.

Option 3. You do not know where it came from.

Option number one is based on science. Science says there was a Big Bang that occurred randomly and the Universe is the result of a chemical reaction that evolved into our current Universe.

Option number two is based on a belief that a Creator caused the Universe to take form. Every religion is based on this option.

Option number three is, "I really do not know!"

So which option best describes what you believe, Option #1, Option #2, or Option #3?

To help you choose which option you believe, let's go back several thousand years. Try to imagine what it must have been like to be a caveman. During that time, your primary responsibility was to provide food and shelter for yourself and your family and protect yourself and your family from being eaten alive by dinosaurs. For the most part, it was a pretty simple life. You didn't have language, but you learned to communicate with pictures and sounds. As cave dwellers evolved, they developed language and learned to make weapons and basic tools for their survival. As they continued to evolve, they realized certain things that they didn't understand or have control over, so they came up with stories and ideas to try and make sense of natural phenomena. For example, if lightning strikes, they had no idea where the lightning came from, so they created stories to explain where it originated from.

They then came up with the idea that there was some sort of powerful force in the sky that was shooting lightning bolts at them. If they contracted a disease, they created stories that said the gods up in the sky were angry and were punishing them for one reason or another. So, it was man's lack of understanding of the physical world around them that caused them to come up with explanations of things they didn't understand. Therefore, these stories became religions.

As these stories were passed down from generation to generation, human beings were still evolving. Some significantly evolved beings began teaching that there was a Creator of all things, and they provided some new stories about how this Creator operated. These evolved beings laid the groundwork for all religions, and their teachings spread across the globe.

The problem as I see it was each of these evolved beings shared a message of oneness with the Creator. However, each evolved being had their own unique interpretation of what the Creator was expecting from human beings, and they shared their "truth" with the masses, and then the masses started sharing those truths with others. Unfortunately, many of the evolved being's messages got lost in translation and were misinterpreted and even completely changed. Yet, the masses concluded that their evolved being was the chosen evolved being, and if you didn't follow their evolved being's way of worshipping God, you could not be a part of their evolved being's tribe. So, each tribe believed their evolved being was teaching the "right" way to connect with God, and the other evolved beings were teaching the "wrong" way of connecting with God.

Therefore, religion is a belief in a story of an evolved being that came to teach human beings how to connect to the Creator. The downside of religion is that they promote exclusivity. If you do not believe in their teachings, you are seen as different and separate from that particular group. In other words, if you do not believe in what they believe, you cannot be a part of their tribe. This is the core essence of religion.

On the other hand, you have spirituality. Spirituality suggests that several evolved beings have walked the earth, and each one shared the same message. Their primary message is that there is a Divine Creator of the Universe, and every human being has equal access to this Creator. Being spiritual but not religious means recognizing that all religions originate from the same source and lead to the same place. Therefore, you accept that some people may believe in a different God other than yours, but that doesn't mean they can't be a part of your tribe. Spirituality is all-inclusive and welcomes all human beings into one Universal tribe.

There was a time when I believed in option #1. As I mentioned earlier, I concluded there was no such thing as God, and I held firm to the belief that science had the answer to everything, and if it couldn't be proved by science, it simply wasn't real. But then I made a paradigm shift. I changed my rigid way of thinking by researching the different religions and coming to my own conclusions and beliefs about God.

To provide you with some fuel for contemplation, I'd like to share some things I've learned that confirm for me that science and spirituality actually go together. I realize that some people may not believe this, but I will assume you are open-minded enough to believe what I am about to share since you're still reading.

Let's go back to the quote, "everything is energy." There is a scientific process called reductionism, which means you can take anything and reduce it down to its smallest component to know exactly what it is made of. There was a time when scientists thought the smallest particle of matter was the atom, so they concluded that the atom was the building block of all matter. As science evolved and technology increased, they realized the atom wasn't the smallest particle of matter. When they broke down everything into its smallest component, they realized that everything was actually composed of energy. In other words, nothing is actually solid. It's energy vibrating at different speeds, and as this energy slows down, it becomes solid matter. Dr. Joe Dispenza explained it this way, "If you stripped an atom down to its raw essentials, all that exists is energy and information, but the atom is not without design. Even at that quantum level, there exists a structure and orderliness, so there must be some intelligence or force that is unifying and ordering them."

So, what is this intelligence or force, and where did it come from?

Once again, this is the million-dollar question. Did this energy and intelligence randomly appear or did "something" cause it to appear?

As a result of my own research, I have come to some conclusions on my own that I would like to share with you. To fully grasp what I'm about to share, it may require you to create a new paradigm on what you believe about how the Universe began.

I'd like you to try to imagine complete darkness and emptiness. Put another way, try to imagine complete nothingness. In this nothingness, nothing exists. There is no light or darkness, or even time. It is pure nothingness. Can you imagine it? Now try to imagine that all of a sudden, something came from nothing. If you believe in science, the instant that something came from nothing was called the Big Bang. If you're religious, it was in that moment that God said, "Let there be light." Either way, the point here is at first, there was nothing, and then there was something. If you choose to see this event from a scientific perspective, how would you explain that? If there was absolute nothingness and then something came from nothing, that means the nothingness was actually something because it would be impossible for something to come from nothing. Are you still with me here? Think deeply about that. How could something come from nothing? I would like to propose that the nothingness is actually something, and that something could be called Pure Consciousness, Divine Intelligence. You could even call it Love, which is the highest vibration in the Universe. If you're religious, you can call it God. As I see it, it is the Source of all things. Everything in the Universe arises from this Divine Intelligence. The instant something came from nothing, an energy was released and there is an intelligence that drives this energy. The intelligence that drives this energy is called evolution. Evolution is the process through which Divine Intelligence evolves to deeper and deeper levels of complexity and this is an ongoing process that will continue throughout eternity.

This energy is within you, and true spirituality is developing an intimacy with and connection to this energy. You do not have to be religious to connect to this energy. Even if you do not believe in this energy, it is still there. Each religion is supposed to help you recognize this energy within you. Unfortunately, most religions get caught up in religious dogma and doctrine and fail to teach you the truth about accessing this energy.

This answers my question of where was God before the Universe began? God was everywhere because God is everything. If God were a human being, where would he/she have been before the Universe began? Hmmm?

I do not believe we can fully grasp exactly what God is in our limited human minds. By choosing to see God as Love, Divine Intelligence or Pure Consciousness, it allows us to grasp the idea of God and yet it doesn't fully explain what God truly is. It's like trying to imagine how long eternity is. Eternity is forever. It never stops. So is God; it is everything and nothing at the same time. It doesn't come to an end.

Now that I've shared how I see God, I'd like to share another thing I've learned about God and the Holy Trinity. Have you ever had someone try to explain the Holy Trinity to you? The Trinity states that there is The Father, The Son, and The Holy Spirit, yet they are all supposed to be the same thing. How is that possible? This is incredibly confusing, and I definitely had difficulty understanding it based on traditional Christianity, so I would like to share my perception of the Holy Trinity.

To start, let's take a look at Genesis Chapter 1 verse 26. "Then God said, "Let us make man in our image, in our likeness, and let them rule over the fish of the sea and the birds of the air, over the livestock, over all the earth and over all the creatures that move along the ground."

Let me preface this explanation with a little caveat. I do not believe in the literal interpretation of the bible. I believe in the metaphysical interpretation. This means the stories in the bible are metaphorical, allegorical, and not written to be taken literally but to be understood spiritually and metaphorically. Therefore, each story provides us with an opportunity to learn something about ourselves to help us grow into the best version of ourselves.

One question I could never get a minister to answer was based on that quote from Genesis 1:26. Why did God say, "Let "us" make man in "our" image?" Who was he referring to when he said that? Why didn't he say let me make man in my image?

I've never had anyone explain this to me, so I'm certain someone reading this has the same question, so now I'd like to share my answer.

Let's go back to the beginning. Remember when I said there was nothing, and then all of a sudden, there was something? The nothingness was God or Pure Consciousness. The instant something came from nothing, something was "born." That something which was born could be referred to as an energy. Since the bible was written by men from a patriarchal point of view, we use the term "Father," but in reality, "Mother" would have been more appropriate since men do not give birth, but for the sake of this discussion, we will leave that alone. So, the "Father," which is God or Divine Intelligence, gave birth to an energy which we will call its son. If you practice Christianity, you would call this son Christ. If you follow the Tao, you would call this son Chi, and if you're Native American, you would call this son Catori. Regardless of what you call it, it is an energy that originated from the Father or Creator. So now you have the father and the son, but what about the Holy Spirit? The Holy Spirit is the individual expression of the son.

Think of it this way. There is a spark of divinity in every human being. You have it, I have it, everyone has it. This spark, this energy, is divine, and it is your birthright. This spark, which was birthed by the Father and expressed by the son, needed a way to be expressed, so God created man/woman to be the divine expression of itself.

Here is a simple story to illustrate what I mean.

Once upon a time, God was sitting up in heaven looking down at the earth at human beings with a few of his angels when he became overwhelmed with pride. "Human beings are without question my greatest creations. I want to give them something that I didn't give to any other creatures on earth; I want to give them a part of me. But I don't want to just give it to them; I want them to earn it so they will truly appreciate this divine gift. So, I need to figure out a place to put it where they will have to put forth some effort to find it. Where do you think I should put it?

One of the angels spoke up and said, "I know where you can put it. Why not put it on top of the tallest mountain? God thought about it for a moment, and then he said, "I don't think that's a good idea. Human beings will easily climb the highest mountain and find this gift."

Then another angel spoke up, "I know where to hide it. Why not put it at the bottom of the ocean? Surely it would be difficult for man to find it there."

Once again, God thought about it and said, "I don't think so. Human beings are naturally curious, and I don't think they would have any problems finding it at the bottom of the ocean."

Then another angel spoke up, "Why not place it amongst the stars? Surely the human beings would find it difficult finding it among the stars."

God pondered the idea for a moment and responded the same way. "Human beings are ingenious and adventurous. I don't think it would be hard for them to find it among the stars.

Then another angel walked up to God and said, "I know the perfect place for you to hide it. I am certain it would be the last place human beings would ever look. Why not put your divine spark inside of them?"

All of a sudden, a huge smile came across God's face. "That is brilliant! What a great idea. I agree with you totally, so I will place my divine spark inside of every human being, and it will be up to them to find it."

This story serves as a perfect metaphor for what the Holy Spirit is. It is a divine spark of God which gives us access to God in our own unique individual way, and it is our responsibility to find it. No one can find it for us.

One of my favorite quotes is, "If you don't go within, you will always go without." Therefore, if you are unwilling to look within your own heart and mind, you will never find God. Most religions have promoted the idea that God is somewhere outside of you, but the truth is, God has always been inside of you.

Going back to the story I shared about God looking down on earth at human beings and being proud of his creations, God came up with the perfect plan to find a way to express itself on earth. In Genesis 1:27, it says, "So God created man in his own image, in the image of God he created him; male and female he created them." Verse 28 says, "God blessed them and said to them: Be fruitful and multiply; fill the earth and subdue it. Rule over the fish of the sea and the birds of the air and over every living creature that moves on the ground."

The way I interpret those two verses is, God made it clear that human beings were its greatest creation. They were given a divine part of God, and therefore, they had dominion over all other creations. Looking at it from a metaphysical perspective, human beings are divine individual expressions of God.

Think of it this way.

Take a moment and think about the ocean. If you stand on a beach and look toward the horizon, it looks infinite, it looks beautiful, it looks powerful, and it looks majestic. Now imagine that you have a jar, and you walk to the ocean and scoop up a jar of ocean. The jar of ocean has the exact same qualities, characteristics, and attributes of the ocean.

It is, in fact, the ocean. There is no difference. But can the jar of ocean be the ocean in its totality? No! It is an individual expression of the ocean, but it cannot be the entire ocean. And yet, there is absolutely no difference.

This is another way to see God. God is the ocean, and you are an individual expression of God. You have all of the same qualities, characteristics, and attributes of God, but you could never be God in its totality.

Put another way, you are a divine personality in the mind of God. As personalities in the mind of God, God communicates with us through divine ideas. Ideas are the currency of the Universe, and when you learn to quiet the noise of your mind and move into the silence of your heart, then you will hear the voice of your soul, which are the divine ideas that come directly from God. I'll be sharing more about this in the next chapter.

I'd like to close this chapter with a very important question. As a matter of fact, it's possibly the most important question you've ever been asked. So when I ask the question, I want you to take a moment and truly think about it before you answer. Spend some time in deep contemplation, and then answer the question as honestly as you can. Try not to allow other people's opinions or what you have been taught to believe to influence your answer. Listen to your own heart and mind and answer truthfully. No one needs to know your answer except you.

Are you ready?

What are your beliefs about God?

Notice I didn't ask you if you believe in God; I asked what your beliefs about God are. For some people, they may not believe God exists. For other people, they may have a very strong belief in God. Some may believe in an anthropomorphic god sitting in heaven, taking notes of their lives and waiting for them to die to see if they can get into heaven. Others may believe in a God of love who loves them unconditionally and accepts them with open, loving arms and showers them with grace.

So if you truly want to know what type of God you believe in, let me suggest you simply take a deep look at your life right now, and you will find your answer. Always remember, your belief about a thing creates your experience of that thing. If you believe in an angry, judgmental God to whom you have to repent of your sins to try and get into heaven, chances are your life is filled with fear and anxiety. On the other hand, if you believe in a God of love, your life could be filled with joy, inner peace, and happiness.

But ultimately, your beliefs about God will always create your experience of God, so it's important to be really clear about what you believe. I am convinced most people really do not know what they believe about God. They may know what they were taught to believe about God through their families and cultures, but they have never really questioned or challenged those beliefs. They have simply accepted beliefs that may have been passed down for generations, and they are absolutely convinced that their beliefs are the "right" beliefs and anyone who doesn't believe what they believe is "wrong."

It is now up to you to decide how you see God. I hope this chapter has provided you with some fuel for contemplation and some insights that will support you in creating an intimate connection to a power greater than yourself.

Rest assured, when you do, your life will become miraculous!

*"I no longer believed in the idea of soul mates, or love at first sight. But I was beginning to believe that a very few times in your life, if you were lucky, you might meet someone who was exactly right for you. Not because he was perfect, or because you were, but because your combined flaws were arranged in a way that allowed two separate beings to hinge together."*

**— Lisa Kleypas, Blue-Eyed Devil**

# CHAPTER 4
## Embrace Connection

D O YOU REMEMBER what it felt like when you had your first crush? When you were first attracted to someone you really liked outside of your immediate family? Did your heart flutter when you saw them or thought about them, or maybe when you received a Valentine's Day card or a simple note that they liked you?

I definitely remember my first crush. I was in the first grade, and her name was Marilyn. I remember how I used to stare at her in class and daydream about being with her when I was only 7 years old. Although this was more than 55 years ago, I can still remember the feeling of having my first crush. Even now, as I reflect on my childhood, just thinking of her brings a smile to my face. I often wonder what happened to her and have even attempted to find her on social media with no success. But I will always remember her and keep a special place in my heart for her.

My second crush occurred in junior high, when I met my first girlfriend. Her name was Julie, and I thought she was the most beautiful girl in the world. Initially, I didn't have the courage to tell her how I felt about her, but she knew that I liked her. One day while we were in the library, I was staring at her, and she got up from her table and walked over to me. As she walked over toward me, my heart was beating extremely fast, and I was very nervous because I was afraid I wouldn't know what to say to her. When she got close to me, she leaned over and whispered in my ear, "You wanna screw?" I was shocked and embarrassed because my teenage mind went into overdrive, thinking she wanted to have sex with me. As I sat there in shock, she reached in her pocket, pulled out a screw, and set it on the table. She then burst out laughing and ran back to her table. I was embarrassed at first, but then I felt relief. As she sat across the room smiling, I knew she actually liked me, and it gave me the courage to ask her out, and we began dating. She was my first love, and she will always have a special place in my heart. We are still friends 48 years later.

My third crush was my high school sweetheart Shannon. We shared that teenage infatuated type of love that you may see in the movies. Her father didn't approve of our relationship and did everything he could to keep us apart, yet we found a way to be together. No matter what obstacle was put in front of us, we found a way to be together. I have very fond memories of hanging out on the weekends with her and going to the beach, which was her favorite thing to do. One of my fondest memories was driving around town in my brother's brand new Ford Thunderbird and having her sitting next to me with her head on my shoulder as we drove around town listening to our favorite love songs.

Those were the good old days!

So what about you? Do you remember your first crush and how you felt when you were a teenager? What did it feel like? Does it bring back wonderful memories for you?

One of the amazing things about teenage love is a feeling of connection. Maybe it's because our hearts are wide open and haven't been closed off because of pain or betrayal. Or maybe it's because we are wired for love and connection, and relationships give us the opportunity to share our love with others.

Either way, teenage love feels amazing!

But is it possible for us to feel that type of love as adults? Can we experience the emotional connection of a teenager as an adult? I believe the answer is yes!

Now the question becomes, why is it so difficult for us to do it? Why are so many people unhappy in their relationships? Why do we struggle with relationships, and why are they sometimes so painful? Why do approximately 50 percent of marriages end in divorce?

If you asked twenty relationship experts these questions, you would possibly receive twenty different answers. Since I am not a relationship expert, I would like to share some insights on how I was able to bounce back from divorce and find the woman of my dreams to whom I've been happily married for the past twenty years. I'm living proof that it's possible to have that teenage type connection, and you can create a rewarding and fulfilling relationship at any age.

Take some time to think about what I'm about to share because I'm certain my story is similar to your story. Use my story as a teachable moment to help you gain some insights into creating the relationship of your dreams.

Here is my story:

After my divorce, the first words out of my mouth were, "I am never going to get married again."

Sound familiar? Of course, my male ego kicked in and rationalized it by saying that I was now free to play the field. The truth was, I didn't want to experience the pain of divorce again, so I was unconsciously setting myself up to avoid that pain as I went into isolation and threw myself into my work. I didn't date for several months because I felt like I had this huge D stamped on my forehead.

The most painful part of my divorce was the experience of failure. I had never really failed at anything so significant in my life, and this was a major blow. Of course, there's the embarrassment and humiliation of telling all your friends and family that you failed, which really hurt.

After several months, I decided that it was my responsibility as a man to be in a relationship. I never admitted that I was lonely and wanted some companionship. I rationalized it by telling myself that a real man should be in a relationship. That way of thinking was partly to blame for my relationship failures.

Since I had concluded it was my responsibility as a man to be in a relationship, I decided to try dating. Since I have never been shy, finding a date was relatively easy, but my first relationship after my divorce was a complete disaster.

The woman I was dating was very supportive. She tried to get me to open up to her, but at the time, there was still too much pain from my divorce. She knew that I wasn't ready to be involved in an emotional relationship, and when she tried to relay that to me, I became extremely defensive. I told her that I had laid the ground rules early, and she had agreed to adhere to them.

The ground rules were as follows:

Rule 1: I have no problem with monogamy, so I expect the same from you.

Rule 2: I love great conversation, so be ready to discuss anything.

Rule 3: I have a great sense of humor and love to laugh, so be prepared to giggle.

Rule 4: I love to support people, so know that you can count on me to be there for you. So feel free to say whatever you feel.

Rule 5: I do not want any emotional attachment. You can lean on me, but don't expect that to be reciprocated. Breaking this rule overrides all other rules and will result in the termination of this relationship.

When Rule #5 was broken, I would do something that would cause women to leave. Of course, I blamed her, but I was the problem, not her.

That relationship lasted approximately two months.

The next relationship lasted about six months, but she broke Rule #5 and decided to leave the relationship because she said I was emotionally unavailable.

I was getting tired of this relationship game and had almost concluded there was no such thing as a good relationship. As far as I was concerned, it was a societally forced phenomenon designed to cause massive amounts of pain. So I chose not to participate for a while.

After a few months, I gathered some new insights and decided to give relationships one more try. A very good friend had set me up on a blind date. I trusted her judgment, so I figured I didn't have much to lose.

My date and I met at a restaurant. I was very impressed by her physical appearance. She was extremely attractive, and after our conversation began, I realized she was intelligent and confident also. After a three-hour conversation, we decided to see each other again. As I left the restaurant, I was glad I hadn't given up on relationships. A part of me knew that she was a very special lady. We started spending a lot of time together, and for the first time in what seemed like years, I had something to be happy about. She was wonderful. With her, I could be myself, and we spent a lot of time just being silly. Our situations were very similar, and we had a lot of things in common. Then I remembered how my other relationships had turned out, and I knew I needed to lay down my ground rules. To my surprise, she had no objections to any of them. As a matter of fact, she had the same rules herself.

Boy, was I happy! This was the perfect relationship, in my opinion. I didn't have to risk being hurt emotionally, and I had the freedom to do as I pleased. It just didn't get any better than that.

Things were going extremely well, although we agreed that we could see other people, we spent most of our free time together. Of course, when you spend quality time with someone the way we did, there is no way you can avoid developing some emotional attachment. And that is exactly what started to happen. I truly loved being with her. I began to fall in love with her but couldn't tell her that because I had set the ground rules, and I knew they worked both ways. I didn't want to risk losing her, so I kept my feelings to myself.

Then one night, while we were together, she embraced me and said, "I love you, Michael." Although I felt the same way, I reacted totally differently.

"Why did you have to say that?" I asked. "Because I mean it, that's why," she responded.

"But you know the ground rules. We both agreed that there would be no emotional bonds between us."

"I don't care about the damn ground rules, I've been trying to keep how I feel about you inside, but I can't do it anymore. If that's a problem for you, then I'm sorry. But I can no longer hide how I feel about you. We've spent the last year pretending to be just friends, but you and I know that it's a lot deeper. Do you think that I'm just having sex with you? Well, I'm not, I'm making love to you, and they're not the same. So, be totally honest, how do you feel about me?"

"Well, I didn't mean it to happen this way, but I love you too. It's been a long time since I've been happy, and you have been the source of that happiness. I've wanted to say 'I love you,' but I was afraid that it would scare you away. I'm really glad that you shared how you feel about me because now I can do the same."

That's what my heart wanted to say, but this is what came out because of my past failed relationships and my fear of getting emotionally close.

"I really like you a lot, but I'm not ready for any type of commitment. I realize we have fun together, but I've got a lot of things to deal with right now. The last thing I need to deal with is the complexities of a committed relationship. Remember, we both agreed on that at the beginning."

"I don't give a damn about what we agreed on at the beginning. I'm talking about right now. How do you feel right now? I'm not asking for a committed relationship; I'm not asking to take up any more of your time; I'm not going to make your life any more complex than it is right now. I simply want to know how you feel at this very moment. Would you please give me an honest answer?"

"I don't know. I really don't want to talk about this right now. Why did you have to bring this up in the first place? Everything was perfect. Now you've ruined everything."

"I haven't ruined or changed anything. I'm asking you a very simple question. Do you love me?"

"I honestly don't know. I enjoy your company, and I look forward to our times together. But I honestly don't know if I love you or not."

There was silence, and I knew I had just lost the woman I really loved. As I lay beside her, my heart wanted to tell her, but the words

## Chapter 4: Embrace Connection

would not come out of my mouth. I felt a deep sadness, and I knew it was the last time we would be together. I tried to hold her, but she was as cold as ice. I knew I had no one to blame but myself.

At the time, I had no idea why I couldn't tell her how I felt. But after addressing my emotional issues, I've realized that the reason I couldn't tell her how I felt was because of my fear of intimacy. I was afraid that if I told her how I felt, she would ultimately do as all the other women had done in my life: leave! The sad part about that was she didn't want to leave. She honestly loved me and wanted nothing more than to share her love with me. I was the one that pushed her away.

After that night, she decided to break up with me. I was heartbroken, but I never told her how I really felt. I knew I was to blame, but I honestly didn't know what to do.

So I did what I was comfortable with. I blamed her for everything. I rationalized that I was a good man, and she was the one who was wrong for leaving a good man.

But once again, I was all alone.

By now, I was really frustrated with relationships. I couldn't figure out how to make them work, and I was becoming bitter toward women for my inability to create a loving, committed relationship.

And then I received a miracle. I was having a pity party with a very good female friend of mine, and I was venting my frustrations to her.

The conversation went something like this.

Me: "You women are always talking about how difficult it is to find a good man, but why do you women always leave good men once you find them?"

Her: "What do you mean, Michael?"

Me: "Well, the last few women I've dated have all said the same thing when they broke up with me. Each of them has said they care too much about me to stay in the relationship. That makes no sense to me. How can you care about someone and leave them at the same time? I can't understand that?"

Her: "Is that all they said?"

Me: "They also said I was emotionally unavailable, but I disagree with that. I'm a really nice guy and easy to get along with. I don't understand what they mean when they say I'm emotionally unavailable."

Her: "Well, Michael, you are my good friend, and I care a lot about you. Are you open to a truth bomb that just may help you figure out why your relationships aren't working?"

Me: "Absolutely! Drop that truth bomb on me right now! I'm ready to hear it!"

Her: "Alright, here it goes, be sure to let it soak in before you respond. Here it is: If one person calls you a jackass, you probably shouldn't worry about it, but if two or more do, then you might want to get a saddle. Have you not noticed that you are the only common denominator in your relationships? Maybe the problem isn't the women in your life; perhaps the problem is you."

Initially, I sat there in shock. At first, I was going to get defensive and defend my point of view. But I trusted my friend's judgment, and I knew deep down inside that what she said was true.

As I sat there and thought about what she said, I had a light bulb moment. I realized that if I ever wanted to create a great relationship, I would have to be willing to examine why I was emotionally unavailable in relationships. Instead of blaming the women in my life, I needed to take 100% responsibility for my actions and figure out how to become emotionally available in my relationships.

As mentioned in a previous chapter, to do this, I had to be willing to make peace with my past. I had to be willing to heal my heart from past hurts and the trauma of my traumatic childhood. I had to remove my fear of abandonment and learn to trust that I was lovable and deserving of love, and accept that women could be trusted with my heart, but I had to be willing to remove the wall I had built around it to let their love in.

Therefore, I decided to take M. Scott Peck's advice and take the road less traveled. I committed to learning how to become emotionally available and refrained from relationships for five years while I healed my heart and focused on learning how to love myself. It was a challenging journey, but in the end, it paid off with huge dividends, and as a result, I was able to find the woman of my dreams to whom I've been blissfully married for the past 20 years.

Unlike teenage love, mature love is a lot deeper and gratifying. It's about accepting the other person for who they are, not how they look or what they have. It's about loving them for their souls and loving the essence of who they are. It is a spiritual connection of the soul in which two people create a spiritual bond that cannot be broken because it is based on what's on the inside of the person and not about anything on the outside of that person.

So, what is the key to creating great relationships and having deep connections with others? Creating a great relationship with yourself. This means you are willing to identify any unhealed or past traumas from your childhood or adulthood. The adage is true, "You can never truly love another until you learn to love yourself." So, self-love is the key to creating great relationships.

Now I would like you to take a moment and ask yourself if you see any patterns in your relationships. Remember what my friend said about the jackass. This takes rigorous honesty on your part and can be difficult to accept, but you must understand that the only way out is through you. You must be willing to go through the things that keep you from connecting with others. So you must identify the patterns and commit to breaking them. You may need some support to do so, so do not be afraid to reach out to a therapist or a coach to support you.

Once you've done your inner work and are ready to find your perfect partner, here are a few things you can do to help you create a lifelong love affair.

A guy named David Hawkins wrote an amazing book called *Power Versus Force*. In the book, he created something called a Map of Consciousness Scale.

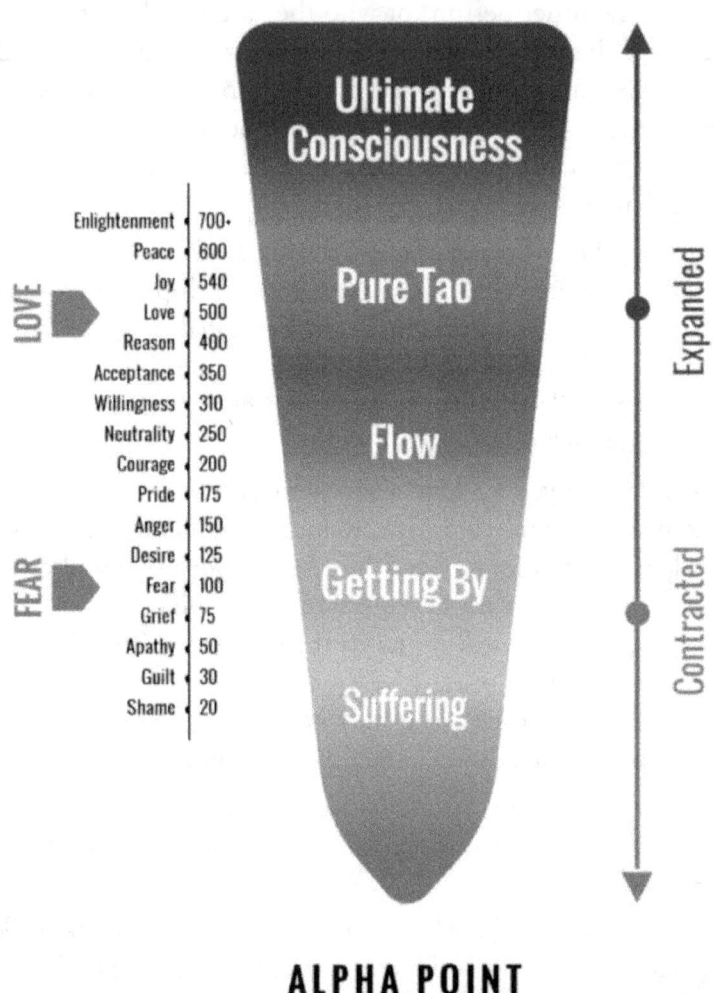

The scale starts at the bottom at 20 and moves up to 700–1000. Think of the numbers as vibrational levels. All human beings are energetic beings that vibrate at different levels, and this scale will explain what those levels are. It's important not to judge the levels as good or bad; simply see them as levels of vibrations that you have complete control over.

According to David, most human beings vibrate at around 200. The point I want to make here is that it is possible to climb the ladder of consciousness to actually reach the 700 level or above if you choose to. To do this, you must be willing to get in touch with how you feel and recognize which level you are currently on.

When I was emotionally unavailable, I was probably vibrating around 20–50. I was so filled with shame from my traumatic childhood that I had very little confidence in my ability to be loved. As I did my inner work and climbed up the ladder, I became happy and secure in all areas of my life. If I had to rate myself today based on more than 25 years of healing and transformation, I'm easily between 600 and 700. My life is filled with inner peace, joy, and purpose, and if I can get there, so can you.

To create great relationships, you must begin by recognizing where you are on this scale and be willing to climb up the scale to increase your vibration. This is why you must be willing to do your inner work and make peace with your past. If you're holding on to past hurts and negative energy, it will dictate your level of vibration and your level of vibration will dictate what you attract into your life.

If you want to attract someone who is vibrating at a high level, you have to be vibrating at that same level. If you're vibrating at 100, you can rest assured you will only attract people who are vibrating at that level or lower.

The key to creating great relationships is first and foremost, having a great relationship with yourself. In other words, it's important to have self-love first before you can attract love into your life. Pure self-love vibrates at around 500, so your goal should definitely be to reach that level to attract that same level into your life.

If you're already in a relationship and want to deepen it, the key is to increase your vibration and your relationship will improve.

It all boils down to how you feel. Being in touch with how you feel and being willing to express how you feel is a surefire way to gauge where you are on this scale and know how well your relationship is doing.

Once you know where you are and are comfortable with your level of vibration, it's important to understand what you are looking for in a relationship if that is what you're looking for.

So, let's imagine you're single and decide you want to get into a relationship. Where do you start? Obviously, the first thing you have to do is find someone to be in a relationship with, right? So, let me share a brief metaphor with you to provide some insights into choosing the right person.

I want you to imagine a beautifully wrapped Christmas present. As you look at this present, you are filled with excitement and delight because the present is extremely beautiful. The present is so beautiful you want to show it off to your friends, so you take your present to a party to show it off. Once you get to the party, all of your friends begin telling you just how beautiful your present is and you are bursting with pride.

After the party, you take your present home and can't take your eyes off it. You can't even sleep because you can't get the present off your mind.

The next day, you decide to take your present to work with you. When you get to work, your co-workers are all mesmerized by the beauty of your present. Once again, you are bursting with pride as you show off your beautiful present to everyone.

One of your closest friends happens to be one of your co-workers, and they come into your office and begin asking you some questions. "Where did you find such a beautiful present? How long have you had it? What's inside of it?"

Now you're beginning to get a little irritated because your friend is asking too many questions. You then tell your friend they should be happy that you're happy for having such a beautiful present, but your friend insists that you tell them what's inside the present. Your friend grabs the present and shakes it just a bit. You become furious! "How dare you shake my beautiful present?" you say. You then tell them they do not have the right to question you about your present, and even though the present sounded like something was broken inside, you refuse to acknowledge that, and you chase your co-worker out of your office.

After work, you take your present home and set it on the table. You are still mesmerized by the beauty of the present, but you can't stop thinking about the sound you heard when your friend shook the package. A part of you wants to know what's inside, but another part is in complete denial and convinces you not to open it.

This goes on for a couple of weeks, and the package has begun to lose its beauty. The wrapping paper is a little torn and the ribbon has fallen off, and you aren't paying as much attention to the present anymore. You no longer take it with you and you've lost the feeling of love and joy that you had for your present. You then decide that it's time to look inside, and when you do, you find out that it is completely broken and it's something you didn't want anyway. So you take your present out to the dumpster and throw it in, and the next day, you start looking for a brand-new present.

This metaphor serves as a reminder of the importance of being willing to look past a person's exterior and look at the interior. Of course, it's important to find someone who you are physically attracted to, but if that is your primary focus, you're looking in the wrong place. When seeking out a new partner, the key is to connect with who they are on the inside instead of how they look on the outside. Just like the story, too many of us are more concerned with how our partners might look instead of who they are on the inside.

This is the reason the Map of Consciousness Scale is so important. If you are willing to look inside a person and find their emotional level, you are much more likely to be compatible if their level matches yours.

This was a lesson I learned due to some deep self-introspection and being willing to raise my level of vibration. The biggest lesson I learned from my divorce was that I had absolutely no idea the interior qualities and values I was looking for in a woman. The first time I got married, I focused on the package and not what was inside it.

So, what exactly should we be looking for inside the package? I believe there are two things we must be looking for if we truly want to build a relationship that works.

1. Shared values
2. Identify our needs

When I got married the first time, I was 21 years old, and I definitely didn't know what I was looking for. In addition to the emotional baggage I was carrying around, I was absolutely clueless about the values I had and my needs.

I have come to believe that shared values are the keys to creating lasting relationships. When two people share the same values around money, sex, religion, children, and ambition, they share a great foundation on which to build a great partnership.

So, the questions you must ask yourself are:

What are my thoughts, feelings, and beliefs about money? What are my thoughts, feelings, and beliefs about sex? What are my thoughts, feelings, and beliefs about religion? What are my thoughts, feelings, and beliefs about children? What are my thoughts, feelings, and beliefs about ambition?

So take some time and think about these questions and then put your answers on some paper. Writing down your answers will give you some clarity on your values. Once you are clear on your values, whenever you choose to date someone, have an honest conversation with them about their values and see if they match yours. If they don't, it might be a good idea to look for another package.

Of course, this is going to take rigorous honesty on your part. You have to be completely honest and truthful about what you value most and make sure you do not compromise your values.

This is how you begin looking inside the package. This is how you begin to learn the essence of who they are. This is where true connection happens.

The second thing you must understand about yourself is your needs. As human beings, we have a lot of different needs, but in terms of relationships, we have four primary ones. According to relationship expert Jayson Gaddis, the four primary needs all human beings have are the 4 S's.

## Safety, Seen, Supported, and Soothed
### Safety

Safety is about being in an environment in which you feel safe to express yourself openly and honestly. It means being comfortable to share all aspects of yourself with your partner without fear of criticism or attack. It also means there is never any threat of physical or emotional violence, and you can simply be who you are with that person.

### Seen

Being seen means we are acknowledged for who we are, and the person we are with is able to see and appreciate who we are. It also means our experiences are validated, and even if we disagree, our point of view is allowed without attack or judgment. Being seen also means being recognized for the unique human beings we are.

### Supported

Being supported means our partners are in our corners no matter what. It means they support us in pursuing our own individual interests, and they give us the space to grow. Being supportive also means standing up and speaking out to us when our partners may disagree with us and want us to see things from a different point of view.

## Soothed

We all want to feel loved and accepted, and being soothed is the feeling we have when unconditional love is present. Being soothed occurs when we feel safe, seen and supported by our partners.

When these four needs are consistently met, love will blossom. Of course, this is probably easier said than done, but rest assured it is possible for you. How do I know this? Because I experience it regularly, and if I can do it, so can you.

I'd like to close this chapter with 10 Keys to Creating Healthy Relationships. Be sure to read them carefully and apply them to your life.

## Number 1:

**Develop a healthy relationship with yourself.** For most people, I can assure you, it is very uncomfortable for them to say, "I love myself." Why? Because for some people, that may sound a little arrogant, a little cocky, a little narcissistic. The truth is, if you don't love yourself, you cannot love another person. It's not possible because all relationships begin with you. The first thing you have to be willing to do is create a healthy relationship with yourself. When you look in the mirror, ask yourself what you see. Do you see someone who's trustworthy? Do you see someone who's lovable? Do you see someone who's dependable? Do you see someone in that mirror you want to be in a relationship with? Ask yourself that question honestly because that's where relationships begin.

They begin with you. If you want to create healthy relationships, start with yourself. Sometimes that means we have to take a break from relationships with other people and spend some time developing a relationship with ourselves. This may be uncomfortable or seem a little weird, but rest assured, it is the first thing you must do. Too many times, we want to point our fingers at the people in our lives, but the fact remains that if we want to create healthy relationships, it always begins with the man in the mirror. We must take complete responsibility for our relationships and not blame anyone else except ourselves. Once we do this, we lay the foundation for great relationships.

## Number 2:

**Make relationships the top priority.** In our culture and society, a man's job has basically been two things: protect and provide. This has been true since the beginning of time. Think about it. What was a caveman's primary responsibility? He was supposed to find a cave to keep his little cavewoman happy and warm, and then he had to go out there to find food and make sure he kept the dinosaurs from eating his family. Provide and protect.

Unfortunately, too many men are still trying to do that. They believe that if they just do these two things, they will be happy. What we really need to do if we're going to make relationships our top priority is to connect; not just provide and protect, but connect. Connection takes emotions, and men often do not have the emotional awareness to connect, which is a major cause of relationship failure.

We usually focus all of our attention on our jobs, our bills, our cars, our stuff, and our kids, but we aren't doing anything to connect in our relationships. We aren't doing anything to deepen our connection.

The sad part is that many men will go through life and work at a career, raise their kids, and do everything they can to keep up with the Joneses. Then they get close to retirement and start asking themselves, "What am I going to do?"

As soon as they retire and they're at home with their wives on a full-time basis, it's total chaos because now they have to connect with their spouse, but they don't know how to do that.

If they had only made relationships the top priority in their lives from the beginning, it would have made their lives a lot easier in the long run. Be sure to make relationships the top priority in your life, and you too will be happier in the long run.

## Number 3:

**Relinquish the need to be right.** That's it! Let go of the need to be right! It's sad, but most people would rather be right than happy. They get attached to being right, which creates disconnection, and then they wonder why they're so unhappy.

Did you know that two people never have to fight in healthy, connected relationships? "What do you mean, Michael? A relationship without fighting? That's not possible!" Yes, it is! I can promise you that it is possible, and here's how: you must distinguish between fighting and conflict. They aren't the same thing. Fighting is about being right. It's about being more concerned with being right than being happy.

On the other hand, conflict occurs when you bring two human beings together who will always have different opinions and beliefs. There's no way you can avoid conflict in a relationship, but you can let go of your need to be right about the conflict, which will instantly transform your relationships.

How often have you fought over something really simple and all you had to do was say, "That's okay," and let it go? But then a part of you took this firm stand that you were just not going to let her be right. We've all done it. It's part of human nature to want to be right. Guess what? It doesn't work in relationships. Relinquishing your need to be right will transform your relationships instantly if you will just be willing to let things go.

At the same time, there will be some things that you feel very strongly about, and you will choose not to compromise. You can do that without being attached to being right. You don't have to compromise your values on what's really important to you; you just have to be willing to say, "I don't have to be right. I'd rather be happy than right." When you do that, your relationships will transform immediately.

## Number 4:

**Be attentive to your partner.** Being attentive to your partner means being in the present moment, fully aware of what they're saying, doing, and feeling. When we do that, we create a connection. When you pay attention to your partner and are really concerned about what they're saying, connection is created. If you really want to create healthy relationships, you must be attentive to your partner; again, it creates connection.

## Number 5:

**Express affection to your partner.** That doesn't mean you have to go out in the street and kiss your wife in front of many people. Affection means that you're in some way affirming that you care about them by touching and acknowledging, and possibly kissing them. Affection doesn't necessarily mean kissing; you can just touch someone and show affection. The key is to be comfortable making physical contact with your partner. Touching is a way to create a physical connection. Studies have shown that infants that are held and nurtured and physically touched are healthier than babies that aren't. It's in our DNA to be touched and held. Expressing affection shouldn't be a big issue unless you're stuck in your ego, so let that go. Express affection to your partner.

## Number 6:

**Say, "I love you," and mean it.** If you truly love someone, why should it be difficult to tell them? When you say, "I love you," be sure to say it from your heart, not your head. Say it often, and mean it every time. If you don't feel it, don't say it.

## Number 7:

**Spend quality time with your partner.** You have to define quality time, but quality time means you move away from all the hustle and bustle of life, the kids, the jobs, the house, and all of that, and you spend time where you're just hanging out. For some, it may mean just sitting on the back porch. For others, it may be going to a spa all day. You have to decide what it is, but it's important that you spend quality time being attentive and connecting with your partner. It's extremely important.

## Number 8:

**Loosen up, let go, have some fun.** When was the last time you laughed with your partner? Just had a good laugh? If nothing comes to mind, something's wrong because relationships should be about fun, not just about stress and all the day-to-day challenges that we deal with. If you want to create connection, you have to have fun because, whether we realize it or not, we all have this playfulness inside of us. It's there. Too many of us have pushed it down so far we've forgotten what it feels like, but we have to bring that playfulness back up and have fun and recognize that it doesn't make you less of a person to do so.

## Number 9:

**Celebrate your victories together.** Life is tough enough as it is. Just look around you. We have all these things going on in the world. Our one refuge should be our relationship and our homes. When you accomplish something or something positive happens in your relationship, you should celebrate that. It can be something as small as a hug or something as elaborate as taking your partner out to an excellent dinner because you got a promotion at work. The key is to recognize that you're in this together, and you should be grateful that you have each other. When you overcome hurdles, it deepens your connection. Have some fun, celebrate your victories together, and acknowledge each other for being there for one another.

## Number 10:

**Count your blessings, not your problems.** Too many times, we focus all of our attention on what's wrong versus what's right with our relationships. When you focus all of your attention on what's wrong, guess what happens... Disconnection. If you're in a relationship, it may not be perfect, but you know this person is there for you, and that's something to be grateful for. Count your blessings for what they do right. An attitude of gratitude goes a long way in deepening your connection in relationships. Make sure you're counting your blessings, not your problems. I can assure you that connection happens and relationships bloom when you do that. That's just the way it works.

There they are, the 10 Keys to Creating Healthy Relationships.

I realize some of you are saying, "Okay, Michael, you've just shared ten keys to creating healthy relationships. I got it, but what I didn't get, what I didn't see, what I didn't hear you say, Michael, is anything about the sex. What about the sex, Michael? You didn't talk about the sex."

Here's a promise that I can make. It's actually a guarantee. I can absolutely, 100% guarantee that if you follow these 10 keys, if you create the connection I'm talking about in relationships, there is absolutely *no way* you won't have great sex.

Here's why: too many times, we think that sex is about the physical act; in reality, making love is about the emotional and spiritual act. When you have your emotions involved, and have a deep connection with your mate, making love is deeper, more intimate, and more awesome.

Because when you really care about somebody, it's no longer just about physical sex. It's about sharing something, sharing a part of you. This whole connection process is about moving past just having sex and making love. It doesn't mean you can't have some wild, crazy, passionate, physical love or sex. That could happen too. What I'm saying here is that we put so much focus on the physical aspect of sex that we miss out on the emotional and spiritual connection; when you do that, you cannot have great sex. If you have trust, commitment, honesty, openness, all those things in your relationships, your sex life, your love life, will work. I can guarantee you that. The question is, are you willing to accept it?

You're probably asking this, "Do these keys really work?" I know they do. How do I know? Because they work for me. If they work for me, they can work for you.

More importantly, I can honestly say that I have this type of connection with my wife. I have a marriage that works because I took the time to learn about myself, I took the time to go through my emotional transformational process, and now it has allowed me to create this type of relationship.

If I can do it, you can do it too.

Embrace Connection!

Good luck!

*The Dalai Lama, when asked what surprised him most about humanity, he said:*

*"Man.*
*Because he sacrifices his health in order to make money.*
*Then he sacrifices money to recuperate his health.*
*And then he is so anxious about the future that he does not enjoy the present;*
*the result being that he does not live in the present or the future;*
*he lives as if he is never going to die, and then dies having never really lived."*

# CHAPTER 5
## Embrace Health and Fitness

DID YOU READ the quote from the previous page? I want to make sure you do not sacrifice your health to make money, so you won't have to sacrifice your money to recuperate your health.

When it comes to living an extraordinary life, it is imperative that you take good care of your health. Health is wealth, and without it, you will never fully enjoy your life to its fullest. Taking care of your health begins with taking care of your physical body.

I want you to take a moment and see what comes to mind when I mention the word "vehicle." Did you think of a car, a plane, or a boat? What did you think of? Now I would like you to think about what might be considered "the ultimate vehicle." To do this, you must first define what a vehicle is. Dictionary.com defines a vehicle as: "any means in or by which someone travels or something is carried or conveyed; a means of conveyance or transport:. I define a vehicle in this context as: "something that moves human beings from one place to another."

Using that definition, what would you consider to be the ultimate vehicle?

How about the 4.8-million-dollar Koenigsegg CCXR Trevita sportscar? Or what about the 4.8-billion-dollar History Supreme yacht made with solid gold? Or maybe you thought about the

150-billion- dollar International Space Station. Surely any of these vehicles could be considered the ultimate vehicle.

So what do you think? What comes to mind when you think about the "ultimate" vehicle?

If you asked me, none of these vehicles would make my list as the ultimate vehicle. For me, the ultimate vehicle is something that everyone can afford, and as a matter of fact, every human being already owns one. In my opinion, the ultimate vehicle is, without question, the human body.

What is truly amazing is that 99% of the mass of the human body consists of six elements: oxygen, carbon, hydrogen, nitrogen, calcium, and phosphorus. They are worth about $576. All the other elements taken together are worth only about $9 more.

So if the human body is only worth $585, why would I consider it the ultimate vehicle?

Remember when I said you are a spiritual being having a human experience? Therefore the essence of you is spirit, and your body is the vehicle that moves you around from one place to another. Have you ever stopped to contemplate the beauty and complexity of your divine vehicle?

Let's look at just a few of the miracles of the human body.

Did you know that your body consists of approximately 100 trillion cells, which all came from the division of one single cell? Every minute, 300 million cells die, but we produce over 300 billion new cells every day, and our bodies are constantly repairing and rebuilding themselves.

Did you know that the human heart creates enough pressure to squirt blood more than 30 feet? Such pressure is needed to pump blood through 60,000 miles of veins and capillaries. The heart pumps six quarts of blood, circulating three times through the body every minute. In one day, your blood travels a total of 12,000 miles.

Did you know your stomach has a disposable lining? Your stomach gets a brand-new lining every four days. Strong digestive acids quickly dissolve the mucus-like cells lining the stomach walls. So your body replaces them routinely before they are compromised.

Did you know that an unborn child already has fingerprints just three months into a pregnancy? At just six to 13 weeks of development, the distinctive whorls have already developed. Interestingly, those fingerprints will never change throughout a person's life. And your fingerprints are your own unique bar code indicating the true miracle you are.

Out of more than seven billion people on the planet, there is only one you! You are a miracle!

What separates the human body from every other vehicle is the Divine Intelligence within the human body. It is the only vehicle capable of repairing itself, and it is also the only vehicle that gets stronger and better the more you use it. No other vehicle is capable of doing this.

This Divine Intelligence causes a single cell to multiply and become more than 100 trillion cells. It is this intelligence that causes a broken bone to heal miraculously, your fingernails to grow, and a single sperm cell to fertilize an egg and create a new life. This is why I believe the human body is definitely the ultimate vehicle.

Let's use the metaphor that the human body is like a car. When you buy a new car, you usually begin by taking very good care of it. You keep it clean, fill it with fuel, and follow maintenance guidelines to keep it running smoothly. Whenever there is a problem with the car, it will let you know about it by turning on the check engine light or making weird noises, or maybe it begins to drive roughly. The point here is that the car will alert you to the problem, and then it is crucial that you address the problem and get it repaired.

The human body does the same thing. It gives you signals to let you know there is something wrong with it. A few of the basic signals it sends are high blood pressure, high cholesterol levels, being overweight, and excessive stress and anxiety. These are all warning signs that the human body needs attention.

So now, I'd like you to take a moment and think about your ultimate vehicle. Do you take good care of it? Are you paying attention to what your body is telling you? Is it time for you to get a checkup to see if your body needs repairing?

Unfortunately, most people wait until something is wrong with their bodies before they will decide to take care of it. It usually isn't until something goes wrong that people decide to do something to take care of their ultimate vehicle.

Like most people, I didn't pay close attention to my health when I was younger. It wasn't until I experienced a life-threatening event that I decided to take my health seriously and commit to being healthy.

Here is what happened:

When I was 18 years old, I received my first full-time job working as a salesman for a building supply retailer. I had always had a very strong work ethic, so being on time, working hard, and wanting to climb the corporate ladder seemed to be encoded in my DNA.

Although I was a very responsible employee that prided himself on never being late, I was still a teenager who wasn't quite ready to give up my partying life. I remember going out to the clubs and hanging out until 3 or 4 a.m., driving home and sleeping for a couple of hours, and then showing up for work by 7:00 a.m. There were a few times when I even stayed up so late that I would sleep in my car in the parking lot at my job and get up to go to work.

One morning after staying up extremely late, I was in the shower, and as I lifted my arm, I felt a sharp pain in my chest. The pain immediately went away, so I disregarded it and headed for work.

Once I got to work, my job was to fill up a lumber rack with some 2X4's and make sure that all the other lumber racks were filled. As I began loading the 2X4's, I felt that sharp pain in my chest again. I disregarded the pain and continued what I was doing. After loading several of the 2X4's, I suddenly felt the most unbearable pain I had ever experienced. It felt as if someone had taken a 20-inch dagger and drove it through my heart. The entire left side of my body went numb, and the pain was so intense that I blacked out and fell to the floor.

When I woke up, there were people all around me. There were paramedics, my manager, co-workers, and even customers all gathered around me, trying to see what had happened. The paramedics then put me on a stretcher and began rolling me outside to be placed in the ambulance. As they rolled me through the store, I remember asking the guy if he would pull the sheet over my head because I was a little embarrassed.

As we were headed to the hospital with sirens blasting and the paramedics connecting me with IVs, I noticed that I was no longer in pain. I told the paramedics that I felt okay, and when he looked at my heart rate on the monitor, he mentioned that my heart seemed to be okay but that we obviously had to continue to go to the hospital for observation.

Once we got to the hospital, the nurses hooked me up with EKGs and heart monitors because it appeared that I had a heart attack.

After approximately an hour, the doctor finally showed up and asked me what was wrong. I looked at him and said, "You're the doctor. You should be telling me what's wrong."

He then told me that he couldn't find anything wrong with my heart. He said that I was extremely healthy and that he couldn't figure out what had happened. He began asking me questions about my diet, if I drank alcohol, and if I had used any illegal drugs. When I answered no to all of these questions, he became perplexed. He then asked me if I had done anything out of the ordinary. I thought about it, then told him that I hadn't been sleeping much. He asked me why not, and I told him that I had been staying up pretty late and partying just a little too much.

When he finally coaxed me into telling him just how little I had been sleeping, he gave a sigh of relief and said he knew exactly what the problem was. Apparently, my body was so exhausted that it literally shut down so it could rest. My chest muscles were so fatigued that they cramped up around my heart and temporarily caused my heart to stop beating. It mimicked a heart attack, although it wasn't one.

The doctor then told me that all I needed to do was get some rest and I would be fine. He prescribed some muscle relaxers and sleeping pills, and once I got home, I slept for almost 28 hours straight.

After that ordeal, I had a new appreciation for my physical body. The fact that my body was smart enough to shut down because I wasn't taking care of it changed my attitude about my body. Since that incident, I have always had a deep respect and admiration for my body, and I have not abused it since. I have been working out consistently for more than 40 years now, and I make sure that I refrain from alcohol, drugs, and overeating. I make sure that I get a physical every year, and I do my very best to maintain my health.

Remember what I said about the body being the ultimate vehicle? This event was my body's way of saying it's time for you to start taking better care of me. If you won't do it, I'll have to. This is how Divine Intelligence works.

And now it's time for you to answer a few questions about your health. Using the metaphor that your body is like a vehicle, has your vehicle been sending you warning signs that something needs your attention? Is the check engine light on and you're refusing to go in for a check-up?

Ask yourself these questions:

When was the last time you had a physical exam?

Do you have high blood pressure or high cholesterol?

Do you have diabetes?

Are you currently overweight?

Do you smoke?

Are you using any illegal drugs?

Do you overindulge with alcohol?

Do you get enough sleep?

Do you feel irritable and anxious most of the time?

How would you rate your current physical fitness on a scale of 1-10, with 10 being the best?

The purpose of these questions isn't to make you feel bad. They are simply a way of noticing if your check engine light is on. If it is, it's time for you to take action and take your vehicle in for repairs.

Here are 10 simple steps to help you take care of your physical body.

## 1. Get an annual checkup.

It is vital for people to get physical exams. People are hesitant to go to the doctor for a myriad of reasons, but the fact remains that getting a physical and early detection of illnesses improve your chances of overcoming those illnesses.

## 2. Watch your diet.

Yes, we love our food, and yes, we love to eat, but we must understand that certain foods are detrimental to our bodies. Fried foods and high-fat foods are the leading cause of weight gain and disease. Commit yourself to eat healthier, and minimize the amount of food you eat.

## 3. Exercise.

You must understand that the human body is not designed to sit still; it is designed to move. It is the only thing on this planet that actually gets stronger the more you use it. Moderate exercise can extend your lifespan, help you lose weight, and help you ward off illnesses.

## 4. Maintain a desirable weight.

If you are overweight, make a commitment to drop some pounds. As you lose weight, you will receive lots of health benefits and increased self-esteem.

## 5. Limit your alcohol intake.

Alcohol abuse leads to all sorts of health-related illnesses. It also leads to depression. Be sure to reduce your alcohol intake, and by all means, never drink and drive.

## 6. Stop smoking, and do not abuse illegal drugs.

Enough said!

## 7. Learn to relax.

There are several documented studies regarding the benefits of meditation. Learning to relax makes you more productive and focused, and it can help you eliminate the need for alcohol or drugs.

## 8. Laugh often.

It's been said that people don't stop playing because they get old; they get old because they stop playing. Never stop playing! Make it a point to laugh and laugh often.

## 9. Learn something new.

Learning should be a lifelong process. Studies have shown that people who keep learning throughout their lifetimes are less likely to experience Alzheimer's and dementia. Never stop learning!

## 10. Volunteer.

Believe it or not, volunteering your time and talents to help other people is good for your health. Studies have shown that people who help take care of others tend to be happier and healthier than those who don't.

These are ten things you can do to help you take care of your physical body. Taking care of your body can sometimes be challenging, but you need to make this a priority in your life.

Once you take care of your body, it's important to examine your thoughts and beliefs about aging. If you pay attention to mainstream media, you may have concluded that getting older is something to be afraid of. I completely disagree. Growing older is a blessing if we're willing to look at it that way.

I recently ran across a quote that expresses my intention to write this book.

*"At age 75, I think aging is getting a bad rap. It's harder to get a job, greeting cards make fun of us, we old folks are seen as responsible for problems with Social Security and Medicare and movies don't have enough of us as heroes. Shouldn't we have a campaign about "old is good" and not refer to wine or cheese in the same breath? Is this a wild thought?"*

N.S.

I love the part where he says "shouldn't we have a campaign about old is good?" That sentence sums up, "I'm Not Okay With Gray!" It is a campaign to let people know that getting older is actually a gift.

I'd like to share a few positive quotes about ageing that should inspire you to recognize the gift of aging.

- "My physical body may be less efficient and less beautiful in old age. But God has given me an enormous compensation: my mind is richer, my Soul is broader, and my wisdom is at a peak. I am so happy with the riches of my advanced peak age that, contrary to Faust, I would not wish to return to youth."
  ~ Robert Muller
- "Here's what I know: I'm a better person at fifty than I was at forty-eight… and better at fifty-two than I was at fifty. I'm calmer, easier to live with. All this stuff is in my soul forever. Just don't get lazy. Work on your relationships all the time. Take care of friendships, hold people you love close to you, take advantage of birthdays to celebrate fiercely. It's the worrying — not the years themselves — that will make you less of a woman." ~ Patti LaBelle
- "Of all the self-fulfilling prophecies in our culture, the assumption that aging means decline and poor health is probably the deadliest." ~ Marilyn Ferguson
- "I've always said that I will never let an old person into my

body. That is, I don't believe in 'thinking' old. Don't program yourself to break down as you age with thoughts that decline is inevitable." ~ Wayne Dyer
- "Aging isn't about getting old; it's about LIVING… Learning that you can age well will actually help you to age better… let's start celebrating and living an engaged life, and stop punishing ourselves for not looking a certain way, and instead, holding ourselves accountable for actually taking care of ourselves inside first, knowing the results on the exterior will be a shining side effect." ~ Cameron Diaz
- "Do not grow old, no matter how long you live. Never cease to stand like curious children before the great mystery into which we were born." ~ Albert Einstein
- "Anyone who stops learning is old, whether at twenty or eighty. Anyone who keeps learning stays young. The greatest thing in life is to keep your mind young." ~ Henry Ford

I think Henry Ford said it best, "The greatest thing in life is to keep your mind young." Therefore, it's important for you to keep your mind young and recognize that age is just a number and your thoughts about aging will dictate how you experience growing older.

According to Dr. Deepak Chopra, there are Three Ages of Man.

Chronological Age

Biological Age

Psychological Age

Your chronological age is how old you are in actual years. You have absolutely no control over your chronological age. Your biological age is how your physical body and organs function. You do have a lot of control over your biological age. For example, a sixty-year-old man who exercises and takes good care of his body will have a younger biological age than a forty-year-old man who doesn't take care of his physical body. Your psychological age is what you think and how you feel about aging. You have complete control over your psychological age. For example, a forty-year-old who worries a lot and is afraid of growing older will have a psychological age older than a sixty-year-old man who doesn't worry and is optimistic about growing older.

Understanding these three ages of man can help you embrace aging more positively and productively. Of the three, I believe your psychological age is most important. There is a lot of evidence supporting the idea that what you think about, you bring about, so understanding your thoughts and beliefs about aging can help you decrease your psychological age, which will encourage you to decrease your biological age.

It all boils down to mindset. Your mindset is the determining factor on how well you will age. A positive mindset means you will age positively, and a negative mindset means you will age negatively.

Which will you choose?

I'd like to close this chapter with something for you to think about. Do you remember the Consciousness Scale from chapter 3? That scale is based on the Law of Attraction, which means like attracts like. Therefore, if you have positive feelings about aging, it will send out positive vibrations into the Universe, which will then attract like vibrations to you. If those vibrations are positive, you will attract positive experiences. If those vibrations are negative, you will experience negative experiences.

So be sure to focus on positive vibrations by having a positive attitude and mindset about aging, and you can rest assured you will attract positive outcomes in all areas of your life.

It's the law!

*"I think everybody should get rich and famous and do everything they ever dreamed of so they can see that it's not the answer."*

— **Jim Carrey**

# CHAPTER 6
# Embrace Financial Abundance

WHAT IS THE first thing that comes to mind when you hear the words financial abundance? Most people will probably think about having a lot of money. If you pay attention to social media, I'm certain you've seen an infinite number of posts or comments about how to get rich, make six figure incomes, or become a millionaire trading Cryptocurrency. It's no wonder that most people will conclude that financial abundance means having a large amount of money. We are constantly bombarded with images of nice houses, fancy cars, exotic vacations, and stacks of money. But is that really financial abundance?

Although having lots of money is a form of financial abundance, I would like you to consider Michael Taylor's definition of financial abundance. I define financial abundance as simply *having enough money so you don't have to stress out over it*. Using that definition, you do not necessarily need to have a lot of money to be financially abundant.

For example, a person who makes thirty thousand dollars a year and is happy and does not have to worry about paying their bills is actually more financially abundant than the multimillionaire who is constantly worried about his money and stressing out over paying his bills.

Therefore, financial abundance is really about having an abundant mindset and being able to do the things you want to do without overextending yourself and figuring out how to pay for things.

So, are you committed to becoming financially abundant? Are you interested in having enough money so you no longer have to stress out about it? If your answer is yes, let's look at some ways for you to become financially abundant.

To do so, you must begin by accepting these two things.

1. There is a Divine Intelligence that permeates the Universe and you have direct access to this intelligence.
2. You are a spiritual being having a human experience and not just a human being having a spiritual experience.

If you can accept these two things, I can assure you that you can create as much financial abundance as you want. There are no limits! To do so, you must embrace four basic Universal Laws put in place by Divine Intelligence.

1. Everything Is Energy
2. The Law of Attraction
3. The Universe is Infinite
4. Thoughts Become Things

The first law you should embrace is **Everything Is Energy**. Science has shown that if you break down matter to its smallest component, you'll find the smallest particle of matter isn't a particle; it's simply a wave of energy vibrating at a high rate of speed. When you slow down the vibration of this energy, you create solid matter.

If you accept my premise that you are a spiritual being having a human experience, the acceptance of this law is the key to your success. Simply stated, you are an energetic spiritual being. As such, you have the ability to create anything or any reality you choose. When you grasp the concept that Everything is Energy, it should empower you to understand you are the source of every experience of your life. Everything that shows up in your life is a reflection of the Energy you're expressing.

This leads us to the next law, the **Law of Attraction**. Following the law that everything is energy, the law of attraction is exactly how it sounds. Based on your energy vibration, you attract everything and every experience good, bad, or indifferent - into your life. If you aren't happy with what is showing up in your life, you must be willing to change your internal energy before seeing anything change in your external reality.

The next law I want to share is **The Universe is Infinite**. We live in a society and culture that promotes the idea that there is a lack or scarcity of everything. This fear of scarcity drives companies to constantly compete with other companies to win customers out of fear that there aren't enough customers. Countries have wars over oil out of fear that we will run out of oil one day. Governments reject immigration out of fear that immigrants will create a shortage of jobs for their residents. Fear and scarcity drive the world's consciousness, but I would like to suggest that this fear is unwarranted. I say this because I believe the Universe is Infinite and there is no scarcity.

When we embrace this law, we come to understand that there is enough of everything for everyone on the planet. There is enough food to feed everyone on the planet. There are enough customers for all businesses to thrive. There are enough mineral resources to fuel the planet. There is enough shelter for everyone to have decent housing. There is enough water so that no one should ever be thirsty.

There is no such thing as scarcity because the Universe is Infinite. These scarcities exist because, collectively, we believe in insufficiency and scarcity. When we shift our focus away from scarcity and place our attention on abundance, we lay the groundwork to build financial abundance for everyone.

Once again, I hear the naysayers screaming, "Oh boy, he's one of those head in the clouds, pie in the sky, airy-fairy, idealistic liberals." To which I reply, "Whatever the mind can conceive, you can achieve if you truly believe." I believe in abundance, and from this belief comes my optimism and idealism. As irrational as it may seem, grasping the idea that the Universe is Infinite and then acting in conjunction with this belief creates the experience of abundance in my reality.

The final Universal Law is **Thoughts Become Things,** and I mean this literally. If you go back to the first law, which is Everything Is Energy, it shouldn't be a stretch to embrace this law. If everything is energy, then that means thoughts are energy too. Therefore, what you think about you bring about. Put another way, thoughts held in mind create likes of its kind. This is the reason positive thinking is so important. What if you knew with absolute certainty that every thought you had was creative? Would you pay more attention to what you are thinking? The good book says, "As a man thinketh in his heart, so shall he be," which speaks directly to this particular law.

Of course, it takes a lot more than just thinking to create financial abundance, but it all begins with a thought. Everything that is ever created begins as a simple thought in someone's mind. So you need to embrace this law as you're creating financial abundance.

The challenge and opportunity is to understand and embrace these Universal laws. You must accept the fact that the Universe is perfect by design, and you are an expression of that perfection. Therefore, you have an infinite capacity to create anything you want. It can be a home-based business or a billion-dollar enterprise, but it all begins with your willingness to accept these laws, dream big and do not let anyone or anything keep you from accomplishing your dream.

Once you fully understand these four laws, the next thing you must do is challenge your mindset and beliefs about money.

I will share some wisdom from a man named T. Harv Eker. He is the author of the New York Times best-selling book, Secrets of The Millionaire Mind.

"Having the right set of beliefs that support your success and financial freedom is critical to achieving your life's desires. But most people have non-supportive, fear-based beliefs about money, wealth and success that were developed by modeling influencers like parents, friends, teachers, the media and even the web.

The good news is that beliefs are neither right nor wrong – they are only beliefs – which means you can change them if you want to. If a belief is not helping you, simply replace it with one that does."

This is your key to unlocking the door to financial abundance. You must first challenge your deeply held beliefs about money, and if they aren't serving you, you must be willing to change them.

So I'm going to list 10 fear-based beliefs that T. Harv Eker shared that many people believe and hold on to. As long as you're holding on to these beliefs, it will impact your ability to bring financial abundance into your life. So take a moment and read this list and see if you're holding on to any of these fear-based beliefs.

1. I have to work hard for money.
2. Money is a limited resource.
3. I can't control if I become wealthy or not.
4. It takes a lot of money to start a business.
5. Money can't buy me happiness.
6. More money means more problems.
7. Money is the root of all evil.
8. I never have any extra money
9. I can either make money or do what I love. Not both.
10. It's not right to be rich when so many other people are poor.

Now I want you to be completely honest with yourself and underline the beliefs you may have been holding on to from this list. The key to changing any belief is to acknowledge first that you have it. So go ahead and underline any of the fear-based beliefs you may have had.

And now I want you to read this list of millionaire beliefs and then replace the fear-based ones with these.

1. I do what I love, I solve problems, and I make a large profit.
2. There's enough money for everyone who is willing to earn it.
3. I create my life and take consistent actions to make it how I want it.

4. Starting my own business will allow me to have no limits on my income.
5. Money gives me the freedom to do things to improve the quality of my life.
6. More money means more choices in every aspect of my life.
7. Money is a resource to do good in my life and for others.
8. I manage my money because when I do, more money comes my way.
9. I don't have to choose between making money and pursuing my passion. I can do both.
10. I can do more for others when I'm rich than when I'm broke.

Changing deeply held beliefs can be challenging but rest assured you can do it. One way to do it is by using the Mirror Technique. Simply stand in front of a mirror and repeat each millionaire belief out loud to yourself. It's important that you pay attention to how you feel as you say them to ensure that you change them. As you say them, simply notice how you feel. If you feel a little timid at first, that's okay. But make sure that you get to a point where you are not only comfortable saying them, but you also have a deep conviction that they are true for you. It might take several attempts to change them, but you will feel a shift inside yourself when the belief changes. Do this regularly and I can assure you your attitude and your flow of money will change.

Once you identify your fear-based beliefs and change them, then you must learn to pay attention to the synchronistic events that will begin occurring. This is based on spiritual principles and might feel a little irrational at the beginning. You must learn to trust Divine Intelligence, and trust has nothing to do with what you think. It has everything to do with how you feel. This is why it's so important to trust your inner wisdom. As Master Yoda so succinctly stated, "You must feel The Force." I'll say this again, having faith and trusting the Universe has very little to do with what you think. It has everything to do with how you feel. Knowing is a feeling. It is the complete absence of doubt. You may not fully understand it, but intuitively you must learn to trust it.

I want to share an experience I had to substantiate what I mean.

During the darkest period of my life, I was completely broke and was living in a run-down, dilapidated building with no electricity. I had a bicycle for transportation, and I didn't have a job. In order to eat, I would sell blood plasma to get money. One day I went to church and the minister was preaching about trust. He said that every adversity was designed to help us build unshakable faith and complete trust that the Universe had our backs.

After the sermon, I was thinking about what he said, and I made an internal decision that I was going to surrender and trust the Universe completely. As I was riding my bike home, I came to an intersection, and a homeless man was asking for money. I had exactly 2 dollars to my name, and I didn't have any food at home. But a part of me said I trust the Universe to be my financial supply and I gave the homeless man my last 2 dollars.

As he thanked me for my generosity, part of me lit up like a Christmas tree inside. I can't fully explain the feeling, but there was a knowingness and a trust that I had never felt before. I intuitively knew that everything was going to work out.

When I got home, I was pleasantly surprised to see a friend who I hadn't seen in a couple of years. He and I had met in Austin, Texas, and I never told him I was moving to Houston. I hadn't given out my address to anyone because the room I was renting didn't have an address. I didn't have a phone or a forwarding address, so how did he find me? It turns out he had been looking for me for approximately three weeks. He was getting ready to leave the country, and he wanted to see me before he left.

Amazingly he received a lead from someone who attended the church I went to, and miraculously, he had found me. He invited me to dinner and we went out to eat and had a wonderful time catching up. He and I attended the same church. We held the same beliefs about God and the Universe, so I shared the story with him about the sermon and trusting the Universe and how I recognized how the Universe was supporting me by him paying for dinner. We both laughed and acknowledged the amazing synchronicities that brought us back together.

After a couple of hours, it was time for him to go. As he was getting ready to leave, he hugged me and then stuck out his hand and said I want to give you a gift. He then handed me a fifty-dollar bill and said, "The Universe wants you to have this." I immediately broke down in tears. They were tears of joy because I recognized how all the synchronicities had led up to that very moment, and the Universe was saying, "This is your gift for trusting me. Know that I always have your back."

Experiences like this continue to happen to me all the time. They are not rational or logical. Countless miracles have occurred which cannot be explained. As I look back over my life and all of the adversities I've had to overcome, I am filled with a deep sense of gratitude and awe for this amazing Universe we live in.

You, too, can experience these types of miracles if you're open to it, but it begins with developing a deep level of trust with the Universe. You must be willing to set an intention of becoming financially abundant, and then you must put forth the effort to do whatever it takes to manifest that intention.

Will it be easy? Not necessarily. But will it be worth it? Absolutely, positively yes! It will definitely be worth it.

Another way to make room for financial abundance in your life is to be willing to let go of things you no longer need. Recently, I drove by one of the largest storage facilities I've ever seen. As I looked at the building in amazement, I thought about how we accumulate all of this "stuff" and end up putting it in storage. Remember the Rollercoaster? The Rollercoaster convinces us that the more stuff we have, the more successful we are. Therefore, we keep buying more and more stuff in an attempt to feel successful, and then we end up putting it in storage so we can buy more stuff. Can you not see the absurdity in that?

To create financial abundance, you must be willing to declutter your mind and your life. This means being willing to get rid of stuff you simply don't need, negative thoughts included. You will be amazed at the miracles that show up in your life once you learn how to let go of and get rid of things you do not need.

So here is a small challenge. Make a commitment to yourself that you will get rid of some clutter this week. You can begin by clearing out your closet and getting rid of some clothes you don't need and taking them to Goodwill. Or, you can clean out your garage, have a garage sale, and then donate the money you raise to a nonprofit organization. Another thing you can do is donate your time; giving out yourself is a surefire way to feel abundant because it fills your heart with gratitude

I can assure you that if you choose to take on this challenge, you will automatically feel more abundant. As you feel more abundant, the Universe will begin to bring you more things to feel abundant about. It could be in the form of money or material things, but the most important thing is the feeling you will get from doing the challenge.

Now that you understand the concept that financial abundance is all about mindset and attitude, let's take a look at some things you can do to help you generate some financial wealth.

Here are three things you can do to help you build financial wealth.

Get a job that pays well.

Invest in a home or property.

Have an investment that pays you something.

## Getting The Job

Getting a job that pays well is entirely up to you. Only you can define what getting paid well equates to. For some, it may be $20,000 per year; for others, it might be $1,000,000. Many of us get caught up in society's definition of financial independence, which usually includes millions of dollars. But in all sincerity, a person could be making $15,000 per year and be financially independent and happy. Take some time and think about this. Ask yourself these questions:

What are my earning potentials?

What is the minimum annual salary I want to make?

What is the maximum I think I can make?

What skills do I have, and how can I convert them to money? What do I enjoy doing?

What am I good at?

What am I willing to do to create the job I want?

Do I have what it takes to be my own boss?

Will my spouse support me in a possible career change?

What the hell am I waiting for? It's definitely time for a change!

Now I would like you to write down your dream job. Imagine if you could have any job in the world. Don't get analytical; just start writing. Be specific about what it would be like.

How much money would you be making? What contributions could you make to society? Will you be a manager? President? C.E.O.?

What kinds of "toys" could you reward yourself with? What would be your ten-year plan for success?

After you finish, make sure you don't leave anything out. If you didn't start writing, ask yourself why not?

Once you've decided what that job would be like, ask yourself what steps you need to take to realize that dream. Do you need to go back to school?

Do you have a great idea for a company you've been thinking about? What game plan do you need to put together to live your dream?

Spend a lot of time just thinking about your dream job and taking notes of the thoughts and ideas flowing through your mind. Pretty soon, the right idea will come (and you will know). Then trust that still small voice and follow your heart.

Remember the power of belief! Whatever you wrote down, you can achieve if you simply "believe."

## Invest In Property

To create monetary wealth, we need to have some solid investments. Not everyone wants to own a home, but it is definitely a good idea to create some assets. Simply saving money is an asset. You should always learn to pay yourself first. Starting a savings account is probably the easiest way to start creating wealth. Ask yourself this question, if I had a five-hundred-dollar emergency, would I be able to handle it without borrowing it from someone else? The biggest problem people have with money isn't how much they make, but how much they spend. I used to make a sufficient amount of money, but I always seemed broke. Speaking from my own experience, I was always broke because I kept trying to create wealth from the outside. Because of the emptiness inside, the external things couldn't fill the void. It wasn't until I filled up the inside that the external wealth became easier to accumulate.

So, the key is to control your spending. Have you ever done a budget? I've always hated personal budgets. As a matter of fact, I used to not even balance my checkbook. But it wasn't until I actually wrote my expenditures down on paper that I finally realized that my outgo exceeded my income. This takes an incredible amount of discipline. But it is definitely worth the effort. You have to be very specific. You have to be willing to account for every penny that you spend before you can really create a solid budget. My recommendation is that, for one week, you write down every penny you spend. That means every penny. Keep a notepad in your car, at work, and home. Jot down everything for one week. I guarantee you will be surprised at how fast the little expenses add up to significant expenses. Once you've figured out where the money is going, you can set your budget and get control of your spending. You can pick up a budget from your local Consumer Credit Counseling Service that can help you.

The key is to create the job you want at the salary you need to have these things without overextending yourself. Don't try to fake it; you will only create unnecessary hardships in your life.

If you decide to take my advice and invest in your life's emotional and spiritual aspects, you will really understand how we sell our souls to try to create wealth externally. My only objective is to get you to think about your current situation, and then decide to change. It's all up to you.

Last but not least:

## Invest In Something That Pays You Back!

I am not a financial planner, but I suggest you speak to one. Obviously, there are hundreds of things to invest in; you simply have to decide to do so. Talk to someone about assisting you in putting together a plan for the future, not only yours but your kids as well. Don't just think about today or tomorrow, think about ten years down the road. Where will you be financially? What do you plan on doing with all that money you've saved up? Think ahead, make plans. Here are a few things you need to be thinking about:

Creating investments that will generate income for you later. Example: I.R.A.s, 401Ks, Certificates of Deposits, Stocks, Mutual Funds, etc

What Ifs? Security Valves

Example: Insurance, Trust funds

Cash generating investments

Example: Rental Property, Business Partnerships

These are just a few of the areas to focus on if you are going to create true success and wealth. Take some time to learn a little about financial planning, and it will pay big dividends in the end.

Always remember, financial abundance simply means that you have enough money, so you don't have to stress out about it.

Become financially abundant!

"We don't stop playing because we grow old; we grow old because we stop playing."

— George Bernard Shaw

# CHAPTER 7
# Embrace Joy, Passion, and Purpose

THIS IS DEFINITELY one of the most important chapters of this entire book, and it begins with this quote from George Bernard Shaw. "We don't stop playing because we get old, we get old because we stop playing." Have you ever asked yourself why you stopped playing? When did you decide that you were "grown-up" and therefore should stop acting like a child and become mature, responsible, and realistic?

Put another way, when was the last time you had some real fun in your life? Not the type of fun where you go out and get drunk and pretend you're having a good time. I'm talking about the type of fun where you take a cardboard box and turn it into a spaceship and play in it for hours. I'm talking about the type of fun where you hang out outside under a street light with your best friends and spend hours just laughing, giggling, and being silly. I'm talking about the type of fun when you purchase your first car and go pick up your best friend and drive around town until three in the morning blasting your favorite songs on your new Alpine stereo. Or how about the type of fun where you're hanging out with your girlfriend or boyfriend on the front porch about to get your first kiss?

Would you consider these things to be fun? What does fun mean to you? What do you do for fun? No matter what you do or how you define fun, there is one common denominator for having fun. Having fun feels good! Feeling good is an energy; it originates from your heart. Do you remember the Hawkins Scale from a previous chapter? Feeling good means you are vibrating at around 500 or above on that scale. My question to you is, how often do you feel good? How often do you walk around with a big smile on your face filled with gratitude and optimism about your life?

My closest friends gave me a nickname; they call me "Michael, Happy Ass, Taylor." They gave me this nickname because of my irrepressible optimism, my positive attitude, and because I'm always smiling. It is a very appropriate nickname because that is how I feel most of the time. I feel happy!

Unfortunately, some people do not believe it is possible to be happy most of the time. A few years ago, I gave a speech titled Living With Joy, and during the speech, I noticed a man in the audience who apparently didn't like my speech based on his mannerisms and frown.

After the speech, he approached me and said he didn't trust me because I smiled too much. He said his father taught him never to trust a man that smiled all the time. When I asked him if he believed that was true, he said if his daddy said it, he believed it. I then asked him what if his father was wrong? What if a man could smile all the time and be trustworthy? Initially, he was defensive and unwilling to change his mind, but as I reminded him of all the adversities I had overcome, like divorce and depression, he opened up a little and began to have a change of heart.

He then mentioned that he had also gone through a divorce and had experienced depression. I then told him that I understood how he felt and why he believed what his father said. I then mentioned that I was living proof that a man who smiles a lot can be trusted. I explained to him that I smiled so much because I was grateful for overcoming all of the adversities in my life. I shared how going to therapy helped me deal with my divorce and depression and how healing my childhood trauma allowed me to make peace with my past, and that was why I felt happy most of the time. After sharing that, he began to smile. By sharing my story, it gave him hope that he too could become happy, and he told me he was going to read my book in hopes of figuring out how he could learn to smile and be happy.

It was a heartwarming moment, and as we finished our conversation, I asked him if I could hug him. He was hesitant at first, but then he embraced me, and though he was a little uncomfortable, I could feel the tension being released in his body. After the hug, his face and body language completely shifted. He then put a big smile on his face, and he thanked me for listening to him and helping him change his mind about men who smile a lot.

So, the million-dollar question is this, "Why are so many people unhappy with their lives, and why have they stopped playing?" Let me rephrase that, "Are you happy with your life, and have you quit playing?

I believe most people are unhappy with their lives because they are trapped on the societal rollercoaster and do not know how to get off. The rollercoaster conditions us to believe that we must have external things to be happy. Because of our consumer culture, we fall victim to materialism and consumerism, and we are constantly buying "stuff" in an attempt to feel happy.

So, it's important to understand that everything we do, we do in an attempt to feel good! Since we generally equate happiness with stuff, we're generally unhappy if we don't have a lot of stuff. Therefore, we work extra hard to get more stuff to feel happy, but as I've mentioned, happiness is an inside job, so we must be happy on the inside without stuff if we want to be happy with stuff.

So why do we sell our souls for stuff? Because we want to feel good.

For example, have you ever purchased a brand-new car? Do you remember the feeling you had when you drove it off the lot and took it out to show it to your friends? Do you remember that new car smell? Do you remember the feeling of accomplishment once you saved up enough money to buy it and then you signed the final papers, and then the car belonged to you? Didn't it feel good?

Or what about having sex? Sex is definitely the most pleasurable experience (when it's good sex) we can have as human beings. The physical sensations are amazing, but the emotional feelings of making love feel even better. Don't you feel good during and after sex?

What about getting a new job? Doesn't it feel good to be compensated for your efforts and get that paycheck so you can go out and buy the things you want and enjoy?

What is the common denominator of these three things: getting a job, buying a car, and having sex? They all make you feel good!

So what happens when we don't have these things? For a lot of people, they feel bad. Why do they feel bad? Because they believe they need those things to feel good.

As human beings, we all want to feel good!

But here is the problem.

Too many of us depend on external things to make us feel good. If we don't have external things, most of us aren't happy. So, what is the key to happiness? Here is what Buddha said, "There is no way to happiness. Happiness is the way."

Since happiness is the way, how do we get it? I believe the first thing you have to do is be willing to get off the rollercoaster. This is easier said than done, but it is doable. Getting off the rollercoaster means you will have to be willing to challenge your deepest held beliefs and assumptions about happiness.

I'd like to share a powerful lesson about getting off the roller coaster and embracing happiness.

Have you ever heard of the Be, Do, Have triangle? Take a look at the graphic below.

Chapter 7: Embrace Joy, Passion, and Purpose

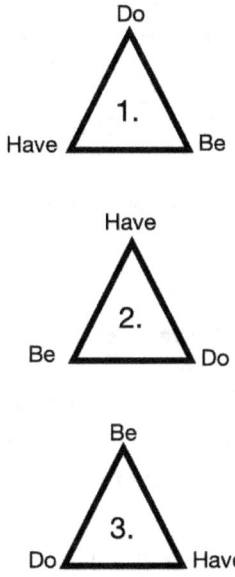

In figure 1, you will notice a sequence most people use to be happy. It goes like this, **Do, Have, Be**. This means they believe if they **Do** something, they can then **Have** something, and then they will **Be** something. For example. If I work hard (**Do**), I will make money (Have), and I will be happy.

Figure 2 is **Have, Be, Do**. If I get a good job (**Have**), I will **Be** happy, and then I can **Do** the things that I want.

Figure 3 is the key to your happiness. You must first learn to **Be** happy, and then be willing to **Do** what you want, so you can **Have** whatever you want.

The key to happiness is Being. You must learn to be happy first before you do or have anything. This is why I keep putting so much emphasis on making peace with your past. If you have unresolved emotional conflict and have not learned how to authentically feel and express your emotions, you will never truly be happy no matter what you do. Happiness is an inside job, and there is nothing on the outside of you that will ever make you happy if, deep down inside of you, there are unresolved emotional issues. One of my favorites goes: "If you don't go within, you will always go without," therefore you must be willing to go within and do your healing work if you truly want to be happy.

Once you've done your inner work, the next thing you must do is figure out what you love to do.

So, would you like me to share how to know when you are doing what you love?

I'd be glad to!

There are three ways to know if you are doing what you truly love.

1. **You do it without the thought of compensation.** When you genuinely love to do something, you never think about getting paid to do it. This does not mean that you can't get paid, it means that getting paid isn't important. You do it because it brings you joy and lights you up. Just being able to do it is compensation enough. So, ask yourself right now, what is something you love to do?

2. **When you are doing what you love, time literally disappears.** Albert Einstein once said, "If you're on a porch kissing a pretty girl, one hour feels like one minute. But if you put your hand on a hot stove, one minute feels like one hour. This is relativity."

    When you are doing what you love, time stands still. As a writer, I can be at my computer for ten hours, and I promise you it feels like ten minutes. When I get into a creative flow, I lose all track of time.

    Have you ever had the experience of losing track of time while doing something you love?

3. **When you do what you love, you want to share it with others.** Whenever we are being creative, a part of us wants to share our creations with others. Whether it's a piece of art, a book, a song or a photograph, we receive joy by bringing joy to others.

    What have you created that you would like to share with others?

Now that you know the three ways to discern if you are doing what you love, it's up to you to figure out what you love to do. If you aren't sure, a great place to start is to think about something you loved doing as a kid. Do you remember something you did as a kid that was fun?

If you can't figure out what you love to do, let me recommend you pick up a copy of The Passion Test by Chris and Janet Atwood. It is a wonderful resource to help you discover your passions and what you love to do.

Some cultures believe that when you die and get to heaven, there are two questions you have to answer before you are allowed to enter. Question 1. Did you have joy in your life? Question 2. Did you bring joy to others?

And now I would like you to answer those questions.

Once you can answer those questions affirmatively, it's time to find your purpose.

Purpose has been defined as, *"The reason for which something is done or created, or for which something exists."* I'd like to condense it and simply state, *"Purpose is the reason you have been created."* If you embrace the idea that there is a Divine Intelligence that created and is still creating this amazing Universe we live in (you can call it God, The Creator, or any other name that you're comfortable with), then try to imagine that this Intelligence created you for a very specific purpose.

If you are truly committed to living a rewarding and fulfilling life, then I believe you must discover your own unique life purpose. I believe something will always be "missing" from your life without finding it.

Before I share some insights on how to find your purpose, I need to begin by sharing why so few people ever find theirs. Although finding your purpose should be a high priority for all, the overwhelming majority will not take the time to discover what their purpose is.

The short and simple, yet complex reason most people never pursue nor find their purpose is that our societal and cultural conditioning has always taught us to always look outside ourselves for validation and fulfillment. Our media convinces us that materialism and the accumulation of "stuff" will make us happy. Still, ultimately, this never works because, as mentioned, happiness is an inside job, and you will never experience it while looking "outside" of yourself. So the key to finding your purpose lies in your willingness to shift your awareness from looking outside to looking within yourself.

If you are familiar with the Christian teachings of Jesus, he reinforced this idea by saying, "Seek ye first the kingdom of Heaven and all things will be given unto you." He then clarified what he meant by saying, "The Kingdom of heaven is within you." This kingdom can also be referred to as your interiority, which simply means the domain of your thoughts, feelings, and beliefs. In order to find your divine purpose, you must be willing to become aware of this domain, and when you do, rest assured that you will enter the kingdom of heaven.

Although I stated, "Purpose is the reason that you have been created," you must understand that purpose goes a lot deeper than this simple statement. To fully grasp and understand what true purpose is, you must understand there are two components to your life's purpose. The first is your inner purpose, and the second is your outer purpose.

Your inner purpose is your true essence. It can also be described as your "beingness", which is a set of qualities and inner attributes that make you uniquely you. Being intelligent, inspirational, creative, and compassionate are all expressions of your beingness. These qualities are always consistent with you, no matter what you may be "doing".

Your outer purpose or "doingness" is how you express your inner purpose.

Take a look at this graphic. It shows exactly how to discover your outer purpose. If you begin with the top circle that says "that which you love," you have an exact starting point. To find your outer purpose, the first thing you have to do is figure out what you love to do.

If you go counter-clockwise to the next circle, it says "that which you are good at." This is extremely important in finding your outer purpose. It must be something that you are really good at. This is where some people get confused about their purpose. Here is an example; let's imagine that you love to sing, but what happens if you have a terrible voice that no one will enjoy? More than likely, it means you haven't found your life's purpose; you've simply found something you love doing. Just because you love to do something does not necessarily mean that it is your purpose. If it is truly your purpose, I can assure you that it will be something that you are really good at.

As we continue going counter-clockwise, the next circle we get to says "that which you can be paid for." Getting paid for something does not necessarily mean that you are receiving money. Although there is absolutely nothing wrong with making money (and lots of it), getting paid for it means that you receive true fulfillment in doing what you love. In other words, you do what you love without the thought of compensation, but if you happen to be able to get paid for doing it, that is simply an extra benefit. You aren't doing it for money; you're doing it because you love it, and when you do what you love, the money will follow.

The final circle says "that which the world needs." When you take what you love and combine it with what you are good at and are then able to be compensated for your efforts, and it somehow enriches the lives of others, you have found your true outer purpose. If you notice in the graphic, all circles overlap and meet in the middle, and that is exactly where you will find your life's purpose. If either part is missing, you have not found your true life's purpose.

Another way to look at your life purpose is to think of it as your heart's desire.

Although every human being has a heart's desire, very few people ever find theirs. There are countless reasons why this is so, but one of the most important reasons is because we stop listening to our own hearts and begin listening to our rational minds. The reason we stop listening to our hearts is that a heart's desire is usually pretty irrational - it simply does not make sense. But when we awaken to our heart's desire, it comes through as an inner knowing that defies logic, and that can be pretty scary. Some people may call it intuition, but it is knowing something without knowing how you know it. You just know it. You know it because it's in your genes. It's in every fiber of your being, and it wants you to discover it. But the people close to you can't see it, feel it, or understand it because it's your desire, not theirs. And they will do everything to protect you from pursuing it because it makes no sense to them.

Unfortunately, most people will not listen to their hearts; they listen to friends and family, who will usually talk them out of their dream. The truth is, they aren't keeping you from your dream intentionally - in their mind, they are protecting you because they care about you. The problem is, you start believing them and not listening to your own heart, and pretty soon, they have you convinced that you shouldn't trust your heart anyway.

Since most of us are taught to be logical thinkers and always be cautious and safe, finding your heart's desire is extremely difficult. Society will tell you to go for the American Dream, which includes the house, the wife/husband, the 2.5 kids, and the 401K, and you'll be happy. Get a good education, go for a safe career that pays the most money, and you've got it made, right? Wrong! It simply does not work that way.

Have you ever noticed how many people do all of these things and are still absolutely miserable? Why does this country have so many problems with addictions and medications? Why are so many people depressed and feel so alone? Why do 70% of people work at jobs that they hate or dislike?

It's because they haven't found their heart's desire. They haven't found their dream!

I don't want you to be one of those people. I want you to find your dream. I want you to find your heart's desire.

So I would like to share some of the lessons I've learned while pursuing my heart's desire and ultimately finding it. I'll begin by sharing one of my favorite books on the subject because it was definitely instrumental in helping me find my dream and unlocking my heart's desire. The book is *Building Your Field of Dreams* by Mary Manin Morrissey, and it's one of my all-time favorites. I highly recommend that you find yourself a copy. It is filled with incredible insights and inspiration that will lay out a step-by-step process for discovering and accessing your heart's desire.

The most powerful lesson I received from her book came to me when I was homeless with no steady job or income and no car. Although I didn't have any material possessions, money, or titles, I had something more substantial. I had a dream. I knew my heart's desire, and I had committed my life to bring my dream to fruition. But at the time, my life was a complete mess. I was in deep debt with no way of knowing how I would get out of it. All the doors that I approached to help get my company started were being slammed in my face. There were times when I even questioned my sanity because everything was going wrong. At times I felt like a complete failure because I had been pursuing my dream for several years, yet nothing had materialized. A part of me wanted to give up, but another part of me knew that I could never quit.

I began reading *Building Your Field of Dreams,* and I couldn't put it down. I had been following Mary Manin Morrissey online for a while, and I knew her philosophy and belief system about co-creation, so when I decided to purchase her book, I knew there was a lesson in it for me to learn. As I was reading the book, a sentence came up that I immediately knew was the reason I had picked up the book in the first place. It was the divine message that I was supposed to hear, and when I read it, I immediately recognized the special message specifically for me. It said:

*"All the while you think you are building a dream but the dream is really building you."* That was it; my dream was building me! It all made sense. All the time I spent reading books and going to seminars to learn about myself and human behavior and personal development was

shaping me to become the man I was born to be. All the pains and disappointments I had overcome were actually building my faith and preparing me for something bigger and better in my life.

As a result of pursuing my dream, I had become better, stronger, more confident, and my faith was stronger than ever. As I sat there accepting the divine message in her words, I began to weep. I was overcome with gratitude and in that moment felt a deep sense of connection to something greater than myself. It felt as though God/Source was sitting right next to me, comforting me and letting me know that I was on the right path and there was nothing to worry about. I then knew that everything would work out and that I was definitely on the right track to fulfilling my heart's desire. As I sat there with tears streaming down my face, I finally experienced the beauty of the famous poem called *Footprints in the Sand*. If you have not read it, I would like to share it with you now.

*"One night I dreamed a dream.*
*As I was walking along the beach with my Lord.*
*Across the dark sky flashed scenes from my life.*
*For each scene, I noticed two sets of footprints in the sand,*
*One belonging to me and one to my Lord.*
*After the last scene of my life flashed before me,*
*I looked back at the footprints in the sand.*
*I noticed that at many times along the path of my life,*
*especially at the very lowest and saddest times,*
*there was only one set of footprints.*
*This really troubled me, so I asked the Lord about it.*
*"Lord, you said once I decided to follow you,*
*You'd walk with me all the way.*
*But I noticed that during the saddest and most troublesome times of my life, there was only one set of footprints.*
*I don't understand why, when I needed You the most, You would leave me."* He whispered, *"My precious child, I love you and will never leave you.*

*Never, ever, during your trials and testings. When you saw only one set of footprints, it was then that I carried you."*

Chasing my dream had been the catalyst of my transformation. Although I began by chasing money and material things, I had now matured enough to recognize that it wasn't about the money. It was about me following my heart's desire and becoming the entrepreneur that I had always dreamed I would become and become the man I was supposed to be.

I believe this is why pursuing your heart's desire is so important. When you find your heart's desire and begin to believe in it and pursue it, you will be guided to grow into the person you must become to materialize your dream fully. Every adversity, every obstacle, then becomes an ally for you. You begin to realize that the still small voice within you will begin to whisper in your ear, and you will hear the voice of your heart's desire, and it will guide you to the places you need to go to fulfill your destiny.

So, let's begin the process of locating your heart's desire.

Finding our heart's desire can sometimes be difficult because of the factors I mentioned earlier. Our rational minds will sometimes keep us from finding it. Our family and friends will also keep us from finding it, and our cultural conditioning definitely plays a part in keeping us from finding our heart's desire.

The only way you will find it is by being willing to go within and discover it for yourself. This is an inside job that only you can do, so let me begin by sharing some things to think about that may help you find your heart's desire.

Since our heart's desire is encoded in our DNA and we show up with it, a great place to start is thinking about the things you loved to do as a child. As children, we rely more on our feelings and imaginations than we do on our rational minds, and if we pay attention to what Albert Einstein once said, it lays the foundation for finding your dream. Einstein once stated, "Imagination is more important than knowledge," and I believe he was absolutely correct in this assertion. When you search for your heart's desire, there is a very good chance that it may seem irrational that you can accomplish it. A part of you will say that it isn't possible, while another part of you will say that it is possible. It's like having two sets of voices in your head. One I will call your rational mind, and the other I will call the voice of your Soul.

Your rational mind is the knowledge you've received from studying and observation, while your soul's voice comes from a much deeper and Divine place. The voice of your Soul is creative and unlimited. It is only limited by your imagination, and your imagination is limitless.

So take a moment and think back to when the Wright brothers decided to create an airplane. Can you imagine how irrational that would have sounded back in their day? I'm sure their rational mind began trying to convince them that it wasn't feasible for a man to fly, but the voice of their Soul said something different. It said that it was definitely possible for them to create an airplane, so they listened to that voice and look what happened. Airplanes, space shuttles, and Mars Rovers were all created because two men decided to listen to the voice of their Souls and pursue their heart's desires.

Believe it or not, you are no different than the Wright brothers. You have a Soul voice within you that constantly tries to get your attention. As a matter of fact, I believe it is your Soul's voice that inspired you to read these words right now.

Do you remember pretending to be something as a little kid that really excited you? For me, I would pretend that I was a businessman and that I was negotiating multi-million dollar business deals in my multi-million dollar company. I even had a secret place in a wooded area close to my home where I would hold these pretend business meetings.

So what about you? Do you remember pretending to be a doctor, a rock star, a firefighter, an athlete, an artist, a celebrity, or an entrepreneur? As you remember what you pretended to be, do you feel a sense of excitement inside yourself? Did thinking about it make you smile?

Or maybe you can't remember pretending to be anything as a child. Perhaps you currently have daydreams of something you'd like

## Chapter 7: Embrace Joy, Passion, and Purpose

to become or something you'd like to have. Daydreams can actually be communications from your Soul that are trying to help you find your heart's desire, so it's important to pay attention to them because they just might be showing you what your heart's desire really is.

So, the first step in finding your heart desires is to answer this simple yet powerful and difficult question: *"What Do You Want?"*

As simplistic as it may sound, most people cannot answer this question because it's a lot deeper than most people realize. On the surface, people will say that they want to make more money, or they want to find their soul-mate, or maybe they want a new house or a new car. But if you are willing to go a little deeper, what you should find is a heart's desire that wants to be expressed through you.

Here is a simple exercise that can assist you in locating your heart's desire. I want you to complete this sentence:

I want...

The key is to write down the first thing that comes to mind, no matter how irrational or absurd it may seem. Don't think too hard about it; just start free flowing whatever thoughts come to mind. Do not sensor it; just let the thoughts flow. Just keep writing until the ideas stop. If you need more space, get a separate piece of paper.

I want _____

I want _____

I want _____

I want _____

I want _____

I want _____

I want _____

I want _____

I want _____

I want _____

Once you've finished, take some time to see if any of the things on your list happen to be something you may have pretended to be or pretended to have when you were a child. If so, pay close attention to that. Also, notice how you feel as you review the list. If something stirs in you and you feel really excited about a specific thing on your list, you may have found your heart's desire.

Unfortunately, this isn't an exact science, and it may take some time to find your heart's desire. But if you commit to making lists of the things you truly want and then listen to the voice of your Soul for the answer, then there is a very good chance that you will ultimately find what you are looking for. Stick with it until you do.

Once you find something that you believe is your heart's desire, you have to put it through the Mary Manin Morrissey Five Essential Questions Test to confirm that it's the right one.

If your dream passes these five questions, I can assure you that you are definitely ready to pursue it as your heart's desire. Here are the five questions you must answer to determine if you've found the right dream.

1. Does this dream enliven me?
2. Does this dream align with my core values?
3. Do I need help from a higher source to make this dream come true?
4. Will this dream require me to grow into more of my true self?
5. Will this dream ultimately bless others?

When I first read her book, I immediately asked myself these five questions. As previously mentioned, I was completely broke without knowing how I was going to manifest my dream, but I intuitively knew that somehow I was going to make my dream come true. As I answered these five questions, it confirmed that I was on the right track, and it filled me with excitement and expectancy that I would fulfill my destiny.

Here are some of the insights I received when I asked myself these five questions about my dream.

## 1. Does this dream enliven me?

Whenever I would think about my dream, I would light up like a Christmas tree inside. There was a passion and energy that would surge through me at the mere thought of fulfilling my heart's desire. Even to this day, being an entrepreneur excites me and fulfills me in ways that cannot be explained in words. It's been said that if you do what you love, you'll never have to work a day in your life, and I can definitely verify this statement. I love being an entrepreneur, author, and motivational speaker.

As an author, writing is my passion. It is something that is in me. I literally *have* to write. While I am writing, I enter this amazing flow of energy that I can't explain in words. Athletes call it being "in the zone," and it is something that is almost magical and defies description. As an entrepreneur, I am constantly challenged to ask myself deeper questions about how to run and improve my business. Though this can be challenging, it's one of the reasons I love it so much. I love the challenge! I am challenged to constantly grow and be creative in finding ways to make sure my business succeeds.

As you think about your heart's desire or dream, ask yourself honestly if it lights you up from the inside out. Does it make you want to get up in the morning? Does the thought of it excite you? The key is to be in touch with how you feel. When you find your heart's desire, you will be filled with passion and energy that will become the driving force of your life. So if you do not feel this type of excitement and energy for your dream, you have probably not found your heart's desire.

## 2. Does this dream align with my core values?

Knowing what your values are is extremely important. Our values are the foundation of how we interact with the world, and they will definitely affect how we express our heart's desires. If you are unclear on your values, it will be difficult to know when you've found your heart's desire. If your values include honesty, openness, fairness, and integrity, then your heart's desire will reflect those values. You must be clear on your values before seeking out your heart's desire.

Imagine that someone says they share the values that I mentioned. They then decide that their heart desire is to create a company that sells illegal drugs. Well, if their core values include honesty and integrity, do you think they would have chosen a company that does not embrace the values of honesty and integrity? Clarifying your values and ensuring that your heart's desire aligns with those values are paramount to your success, so make sure that you're clear on your values and align those values with your heart's desire.

## 3. Do I need help from a higher source to make this dream come true?

You do not have to adhere to any religious dogma or doctrine to accept that there is a power greater than yourself that can support you in fulfilling your heart's desire. As a former Atheist, I can understand if you have some resistance to this particular step. I have come to know that there is a power greater than myself in the Universe. This power goes by many different names, but ultimately the name is irrelevant. What's important is that you develop a relationship or connection with it if you truly want to find your heart's desire. Ultimately, you will have to rely on it to support you in finding and ultimately manifesting your heart's desire.

There is a wonderful quote that says, "If your dream doesn't frighten you, then it's simply not big enough." Having a connection to a power greater than yourself will help you move through your fears and give you the courage, strength, patience, and perseverance to bring your dream to fruition. If you don't need assistance, I can assure you that you have not found your heart's desire.

## 4. Will this dream require me to grow into more of my true self?

This is the true litmus test to see if you've found the right dream. As I mentioned earlier, while you think you are building your dream, the reality is your dream will be building you. If you do not have to grow to build your dream, you are chasing the wrong one. Your dream will definitely take you out of your comfort zone, which is one reason you have the dream in the first place. Too many people stay trapped in their comfort zones and are unwilling to get out of them. They are too afraid and unsure of themselves, so they play it safe and buy into the status quo.

My suggestion is for you to get comfortable with being uncomfortable. There can be no growth without discomfort, so you may as well accept it. If your dream does not cause you to feel uncomfortable, it's definitely not your heart's desire.

## 5. Will this dream ultimately bless others?

Muhammad Ali once said, "Being in service to others is the rent we pay for our room here on earth." This powerful quote speaks to the importance of using our heart's desire to help make the world a better place. I believe that every human being has unique gifts and talents that are given to them to move humanity forward, and finding your heart's desire will unleash those gifts. When your dream blesses others, you know that you've found your heart's desire.

Finding your heart's desire does not have to be some grandiose experience that impacts the entire world on a large scale. Finding your heart's desire means you have found that special contribution that only you can make to the world. In your own unique way, you have positively impacted someone's life other than your own.

Your heart's desire could be as simple as baking pies for homeless people or teaching someone in your neighborhood to read. It does not have to be something that is featured in the headlines. It is simply something that you give from your heart unconditionally to another human being that makes them feel cared about and loved.

So instead of trying to figure out how to get rich or accumulate more material possessions, focus your attention on finding your heart's desire. I can assure you that you will be rich beyond measure and more fulfilled than you can ever imagine.

Of course, there is absolutely nothing wrong with making lots of money and having nice things. Just make sure that you find your heart's desire and do your part in making the world a better place, and everything else in your life will fall into place.

## Good luck!

"If you want to go quickly, go alone. If you want to go far, go together." – African Proverb

The fact that societies are becoming increasingly multi-ethnic, multicultural, and multi-religious is good. Diversity is a strength, not a weakness.

— **Antonio Guterres**

# CHAPTER 8
## Embrace Diversity

According to a Gallup study a couple of years ago, Americans' already tepid review of relations between White and Black Americans has soured since 2018 and is now the most negative of any year in Gallup's trend since 2001. The majority of U.S. adults say relations between White and Black Americans are very (24%) or somewhat bad (31%), while less than half call them very (7%) or somewhat (37%) good.

The study also concluded that most Americans were upbeat about White-Black relations from 2001 through 2013, with the percentage calling them good to any degree ranging from 63% to 72%. The sharp decline in positive perceptions to 47% in 2015 followed numerous high-profile incidents in the prior year of unarmed Black citizens being killed by White police officers.

After improving slightly in 2016 and 2018, ratings of race relations have fallen to a new low in a Gallup telephone poll conducted on June 8-July 24, 2020. The nationally representative survey of 1,226 U.S. adults includes an oversample of Black Americans weighted to their correct population proportion.

The latest poll was taken after the start of widespread protests on racial justice sparked by the death of George Floyd in Minneapolis in May, but before the recent shooting of Jacob Blake in Kenosha,

Wisconsin, and political conflict in Portland, Oregon, that have led to deaths among protestors and counter-protestors.

So, what do you believe? Do you believe race relations are getting worse or getting better? This isn't just about black and white; it's about all races and cultures. Are race relations between different races around the globe getting better or worse?

Obviously, there is no shortage of opinions on this topic, so I'd like to share mine.

On Saturday, May 14th 2022, an 18-year-old white supremacist named Payton Gendron walked into a grocery store and randomly killed 10 black people.

In 2019, another white supremacist named Patrick Crusius targeted and killed 23 Hispanic people in a Walmart store in El Paso, Texas.

White supremacist Brenton Tarrant killed 51 Muslim people in two different mosques in Christchurch, New Zealand, on March 15th 2019. It was the worst mass shooting in the country's history.

On June 12, 2016, Omar Mateen, a 29-year-old man, killed 49 people and wounded 53 more in a mass shooting at Pulse, a gay nightclub in Orlando, Florida, United States. Orlando Police officers shot and killed him after a three-hour standoff. In a 911 call made shortly after the shooting began, Mateen swore allegiance to the leader of the Islamic State of Iraq and Syria, Abu Bakr a—Baghdadi and said the U.S. killing of Abu Waheeb in Iraq the previous month "triggered" the shooting. He later told a negotiator he was "out here right now" because of the American-led interventions in Iraq and Syria, and that the negotiator should tell the United States to stop the bombing.

These four stories alone could make the case that race relations around the world are getting worse. The shocking nature of these crimes highlights the fact that some people hold radical racist views and are willing to murder as a result of those views. When we see horrific stories such as these, it's no wonder most people might conclude that race relations around the world are getting worse.

But are they?

Before I share my views, let me begin by saying in no way do I intend to minimize nor deny the fact there are people on the planet who hold extremely racist views, and they must be held accountable if those views result in them hurting others. It breaks my heart to see so many people senselessly killed simply because of the color of their skin or because of their religion or sexual orientation. Now more than ever, we must work together to find solutions to remove the hate from our world, and one way we can do this is by embracing diversity.

I fervently believe that race relations around the globe aren't getting worse, though it may appear they are. I believe that human beings are still evolving, and Divine Intelligence drives this evolutionary process. As human beings continue to evolve in consciousness, I believe it is inevitable that all human beings will one day learn to accept that we are all the same and eventually (maybe not in my lifetime), racism will no longer exist.

Since I live in America, I'd like to share my answer to the question, "Is America Racist?" As a man who happens to be black and has experienced every imaginable type of racism, my answer is no, America is not a racist country. Are there racists that inhabit the US? Of course! The problem, as I see it, is we tend to refer to America as though it were a person. When people talk about the atrocities of slavery and discrimination, they refer to America as though it were a single person acting out on its own and causing these things to happen. We must accept the truth that America comprises a diverse group of people who make up this great country. So America is simply a reflection of the consciousness of the people who live here. Since the majority of people living in the US, for the most part, have been white people (except when they first invaded America), this country has what I call a *Collective White Belief System* (CWBS). The CWBS has controlled this country for a very long time, but as the country has become more diverse, the CWBS is losing its influence and power.

When people talk about institutionalized racism and white privilege, what they are speaking of is the CWBS. It is a belief system based on white supremacy and superiority that goes back hundreds of years. Another reason for my optimism is the fact that each generation moves further and further away from the CWBS. During the '60s and the Civil Rights Movement, the CWBS began shifting. The civil rights movement pioneers convinced enough white people that segregation and the treatment of people of color were wrong. This was no easy task. Changing the CWBS wasn't easy. That's why there were lunch counter sit-ins. That's why there was a march on Washington. That's why Dr. King's dream speech was so important. In order to shift the CWBS, a tipping point had to be reached, and once it did, things began to change.

So, what is the tipping point? Some people believe that once 51 percent of the population agrees on a new belief, that belief changes the country's collective consciousness. Using the example of the Civil Rights Movement, once 51 percent of white people changed their minds, the CWBS changed, and the civil rights movement was accepted and it changed the country.

Despite the apparent racial conflict that is still going on in this country, I believe that the CWBS is still being broken down, and this country can achieve racial harmony. I believe it's inevitable. There is always chaos before creation, and the current racial chaos we're experiencing will eventually lead to unity. You may be asking why I believe this, and that I am a pie-in-the-sky-dreamer, but I believe that there is divine order in the Universe and that power that is greater than myself is orchestrating the entire cosmos. This Divine Intelligence has an intention, and that is to create heaven right here on earth, and nothing can thwart that intention.

This does not mean that the CWBS does not exist. Quite the contrary. It still exists, and it still influences the minds and hearts of many people in this country. Proof of this can be found in our former 44th president. It can also be found in the racially motivated attacks on people of color. It can be found when white police officers kill black men and are acquitted of any crime, despite irrefutable evidence. It can be found in the disproportionate coverage of negative stories about black men. It is alive and well in this country. Still, as mentioned, I see a light at the end of the tunnel, and I am certain that the CWBS can be changed to the CHBS, Collective Human Belief System in which all human beings are accepted for who they are, and their diversity is celebrated.

It's been said that the first step in solving a problem is admitting you have one. To get rid of the CWBS, we must be willing to admit that it exists. Since the media contributes so much to our beliefs and perpetuates so many stereotypes, we need to acknowledge that the majority of people that control our media happen to be white. They are driven by the CWBS, and although they may not be intentionally trying to hurt black people or hold them back, the result is still the same. They are contributing to the negative stereotypes of black people. So rather than call them racists, I will assert that they are biased based on the CWBS. For them to change that bias, we must continue to bring it to their attention by speaking out against the unequal coverage of people of color and violence. We need to challenge them to showcase the positive stories as equally as they do the negative ones.

The one thing the CWBS refuses to acknowledge is that, collectively speaking, America loves violence. This is evidenced by the movies we watch, the music we listen to, the books and magazines we read, and of course, the news that we watch. Just take a moment and think about the successful movies, music, and magazines in America. The majority of them are overwhelmingly violent and negative. Companies create products and services based on demand; if the demand wasn't there, they would stop creating the content. So who are the people who are demanding this type of content? Since black people only make up approximately 13% of America, you can rest assured that they aren't responsible for this obsession with violence. The violence is driven by the CWBS simply because they are the majority of people demanding this content.

So the key to changing the CWBS is to change the minds and hearts of people who are a part of the CWBS and challenge them to embrace the CHBS, the Collective Human Belief System. This is already occurring.

If you will take a moment and think about it, this country has actually come a very long way in a relatively short period if you put it in the context of human evolution. America is only approximately 245 years old. It began with a single document called The Declaration of Independence.

*"We hold these truths to be self-evident, that all men are created equal, that they are endowed by their creator with certain unalienable rights, that among these are life, liberty and the pursuit of happiness. That to secure these rights, Governments are instituted among men, deriving their just powers from the consent of the governed. That whenever any form of government becomes destructive of these ends, it is the right of the people to alter or to abolish it, and to institute new Government, laying its foundation on such principles and organizing its powers in such form, as to them shall seem most likely to effect their safety and happiness."*

Of course, this country hasn't fully embraced the idea that all men are created equal just yet. If we look at how this country has collectively treated most people of color, it's pretty obvious that we still have a way to go.

As I reflect over my 61-year lifetime here in America, I am extremely optimistic about the future and where this country is headed. I remember growing up in the sixties and wondering why blacks and whites didn't get along. I remember sitting in the cafeteria with black kids on one side and white kids on the other side and wondering why we were separated. I also remember a race riot that broke out in elementary school between blacks and whites. Can you believe that? A race riot in elementary school?

I remember watching television with my grandparents on our little black and white tv and seeing their excitement whenever they saw a black person on television. Seeing a black person on television was a big event that usually resulted in my grandmother calling friends and families to ensure they didn't miss it.

I remember being told to make sure not to be across the railroad tracks on the white side of town after dark because there was the possibility of me being killed by white people.

I remember having a crush on a white girl and then being told that it was forbidden and I was not allowed even to have her as a friend because I could get hurt.

## Chapter 8: Embrace Diversity

I remember the first time I was called a nigger by a little white girl, and even though I didn't fully understand what the word meant, I remember the pain I felt knowing that somehow being black made me different.

But most of all, I remember the sadness and confusion I felt the day Martin Luther King was killed. I didn't understand how someone trying to bring peace to the country would lose his life to violence.

As I reflect back on my life and look at my life now, it confirms my reason for optimism. It is pretty obvious we still have a way to go in this country but based on the trajectory we are on, I personally believe we are moving in the right direction.

As I look at the influence and impact that black people have had on this country, I recognize that we have always been assets to this country and not liabilities. As I watch television and see the infinite number of black people on the screen and behind the scenes, I am inspired by the creativity, ingenuity, and innovativeness that black creators contribute to society.

As I walk around my diverse community, I do not have to fear for my life. I can go across the tracks anytime and be welcomed and embraced by a wide variety of races. In the Houston area where I live, there are over a hundred different languages spoken, and I can go to Chinatown, Germantown, Russian town and a host of other sections of racial cultures. It truly is a melting pot of diverse cultures, and I love experiencing the differences and similarities of all of them.

As I watch television and see interracial couples being featured and accepted through mainstream media, it's hard to believe that only 60-70 years ago, it was against the law for people of different races to marry.

During the early '70s, I was a DJ in Corpus Christi, Texas. At the time, we didn't have any prominent black radio stations. In order to listen to black music, I purchased a radio antenna so I could pick up black radio stations in Houston. I would also drive to Houston and go to the clubs to hear the latest and most popular music and buy albums to take back with me. I was known for keeping up with the latest music, and I actually made a lot of money creating cassette mixtapes. I remember when the television show MTV was launched, and they would not feature black artists. It wasn't until Michael Jackson's Thriller album took the world by storm that they began featuring black artists. Fast forward to today, and hip hop is the most popular genre of music in the world.

Words cannot adequately describe the feelings of pride and joy I experienced when Barack Obama became president of the United States. Most of my friends said I was too optimistic, and they didn't believe America was ready to elect a black president. I wasn't sure he would win at the beginning, but I honestly believed it was possible.

I'm reminded of a quote from Dr. Martin Luther King Junior in which he stated, "We're not where we want to be, but thank God, we're not where we used to be."

This quote sums up exactly how I feel. I recognize we still have a way to go regarding race relations, but the world has changed dramatically for the better, and as mentioned, I believe the trajectory we are on should give us all reasons for optimism.

As a man who happens to be black, I have been accused of being a sellout because of my optimistic outlook. I've been accused of denying my ethnicity because I choose to see life through an optimistic lens. I've dealt with this all of my life, yet I have not allowed the doomsayers and naysayers to change my mind or my attitude about what it means to be a black man in America.

I'd like to share an article I wrote that encapsulates how I feel as a black man in America. It is appropriately titled: The Trials And Triumphs Of A Joyful Black Man In America.

Growing up as a young black male in the inner-city projects of Corpus Christi, Texas, I was acutely aware that being "black" somehow made me different. As I watched television and looked through magazines and books, I realized that the people I perceived to have all of the wealth were white people. When I asked my mom the reason for this, her response was that there were lots of wealthy blacks, but the white people did not want to show that on television. When asked why not, she responded by saying that this was how white people could control the minds of black people and keep them from attaining wealth. Even as a child, there was something about that comment that I did not agree with. I wanted to understand how the mind worked, and most of all, I wanted to understand how white people could control the minds of black people?

As I progressed through elementary school, I remember the tension and fear I felt as I interacted with white kids in my class. At the age of nine, I had my first experience of racism when a white female classmate approached me after a spelling test. In this class, the person who scored an A on a test would receive a gold star, which was then placed on a poster board in plain view for all the students to see. It just so happened that I had the most gold stars of anyone in the class. The teacher would always encourage me to do well and be comfortable being at the top of the class intellectually and academically. After this particular test, the white female classmate came up to me and said, "My mom says that all niggers are dumb and stupid and even though you may have more stars than I do, I am still smarter than you." I stood there in shock and disbelief and was unable to respond. Even though I had the evidence to refute her comments, as a nine-year-old, the pain of her words cut me like a knife. I felt angry, yet ashamed, because this was not the first time I had heard those words. But this was the first time I had heard them targeted directly at me by one of my peers.

My most painful experience of blatant racism occurred when I was seventeen. I was in high school, and I met and fell in love with my high school sweetheart. She was a wonderful supportive, caring person that incidentally happened to be white. When we met, she was somewhat of a wild child. She came from a wealthy family yet hated her father and was into drugs and rebellious. She was a C and D student that liked to skip school and hang out at the beach with her friends. After going out with her for a while, I convinced her to turn her life around and give up skipping school and abusing drugs.

She changed her attitude and became an A and B student. We were extremely close and shared that high school infatuated kind of love that feels so deep that it stays with you for a lifetime. After going out with her for over a year, her father found out we were dating. One night, I got a phone call from him, and it was obvious that he was not happy.

As he began speaking, I knew that I needed to keep my cool and not disrespect him. I listened to his objections and allowed him to get everything off his chest. When he finished, I made the mistake of telling him that he did not have the right to decide whom his daughter should date. I tried to convince him that I had been a good influence on his daughter and that he should be happy that she was doing so well. I hoped that I could get him to understand that I was a good guy that was actually good for his daughter. Of course, he could not hear a word I was saying. He was adamant about the fact that he knew what was best for his daughter, and I was just some young punk trying to take advantage of his little girl. After screaming his disapproval of our relationship for several minutes, he said something that completely caught me off guard. Although I knew he was angry, I did not expect to hear these words, "There is no way that I will allow my daughter to date a nigger. I will kill you before I let that happen." Although the words were painful, it was the venomous feeling of anger and hatred that came through the phone that ripped out my heart. Even today, almost thirty years later, I can still feel the hatred in his words. His anger came from deep within his soul, and it was apparent that his anger wasn't just about me but about all black people.

As I sat there in disbelief, I immediately went numb. A part of me wanted to defend myself and curse at him and retaliate somehow. My initial feeling was anger, which I quickly subdued to avoid getting into a shouting match. Another part of me was terrified because I did not know whether or not he would actually attempt to take my life. But the feeling I remember most after his comment was sadness. I remember a sinking feeling in my gut that was the result of being invalidated as a human being. I knew that he viewed me as less than a man and, in his mind, I was not good enough for his daughter simply because I was black. It was dehumanizing and demoralizing. How could this man hate me so much and not know anything about me? How could he pass judgment on me without ever seeing me or speaking to me? Why could he not see the positive influence I had on his daughter? Why was

I not allowed the opportunity to meet with him and talk to him so that he could see how much I really cared about his daughter and that my intentions were to simply love and support her? So many questions, so few answers.

I share these three true personal stories because, as a black man, I realize that my experiences are really just a microcosm of the challenges facing black men even today. I personally believe that our media still does an irresponsible job of portraying black people in general. The media-generated perception is that being black is synonymous with being poor, uneducated, unmotivated, and somehow a burden on society. Although I do not believe that the media can control how black people think, I am aware of the media's power on a person's perception. Since a person's perception is their reality, the media definitely influences people's minds.

It is my fervent belief that people, in general, are not born racist. Hatred is not a part of a person's genetic makeup. Racism is learned, and people usually learn from the environments in which they are raised. Unfortunately, some parents still teach their children that black people are inferior as human beings, and sadly enough, some black people have accepted this as true.

As a black man, I realize that people will judge me and have preconceived ideas about who I am. I understand that no matter what I do, the stereotypes of black men will precede me, and somehow, I will have to prove myself repeatedly. I know that people will be afraid of me, will think less of me and put the label of a "black" man on me no matter what I do.

So as a black man, what can I do? How do I deal with the multiplicity of challenges that I face daily? Do I throw my hands up in defeat and give up? Do I accept the stereotypes and become just another black male statistic thrown into the ever-increasing prison population? Do I succumb to the pressure, lose my identity, and try to become someone I'm not?

To deal with the challenges mentioned above, I choose to first and foremost see myself as a man, not just a black man. If I see the world only through the lens of a black man, I limit my perception of the world. When I let go of my attachment to being black first, I open the door to infinite possibilities for myself as a human being. This is not a denial of my ethnicity; it is simply an affirmation of my true potential and humanity. This awareness gives me an entirely new perspective on the world.

With this perspective, I can honestly say that I absolutely love being a black man. I have come to this conclusion due to the past twenty-five years of doing my emotional work , removing my shadows, and discovering who I really am. I am now completely comfortable with who I am as a human being, and I recognize that I am a man who happens to be black. I am proud of my racial heritage, but the true source of my power transcends the color of my skin or my ethnic identity.

When I view the world from this perspective, I begin to recognize that although there is ignorance and hatred in the world, racism in and of itself is actually an over-used word in our society that keeps us separate and in denial of our oneness. This does not excuse injustice and oppression for people of color; it simply acknowledges that racism is a disease of the mind. In objective scientific terms, it isn't real. It is a man-made creation that exists only in our minds.

As I reflect on my personal mission statement: "As a man amongst men, I create a world of Love and understanding by loving myself and understanding others." I fully grasp the implications of what these words mean to me. By loving myself and removing any blocks to my awareness, I am able to understand others without judgment. This allows me to constantly be in the moment without being attached to things that have happened to me in the past. By healing my anger and forgiving those who have hurt me, I can be fully present to people in my life. Therefore, I do not think in over-generalized statements and use words and phrases like those white people or them and they. I live in the moment and address each individual situation in the moment. This is the beauty of healing your heart. It frees you from your past and keeps you in the present moment.

My intention is for you to have a new perception of black men after reading this article. The truth is that we are no different from any other group of men. We are loving, caring, compassionate, sensitive, intelligent, forgiving, and courageous. We love our country and our families. We deal with all of the same emotions and challenges as anyone else. We do not all blame society for our challenges, and we are constantly making positive contributions to America. We are definitely an asset to this country, not a liability.

I am reminded of a lesson I learned from Wayne Dyer in which he taught me that I should never focus my attention on that which I am against. Instead, I must focus my attention on that which I am for and I will experience that as a result. So instead of being against racism, I am for unity. Instead of taking a position against hatred, I take a stand for love.

As Dr. Martin Luther King Jr. said, "We're afraid of each other because we do not know one another, we do not know one another because most of us are separated from each other." My intention is to remove the perceived separation and create oneness. This is the driving force in my life. I want to be the change I want to see in the world, and I invite you to join me in creating a world of love, peace, and unity.

In the immortal words of John Lennon, "You may say that I'm a dreamer, but I'm not the only one. I hope someday you'll join us, and the world will be as one."

Won't you join me?

So, what did you think about the article? Do you agree or disagree?

The important thing to remember is that your perception creates your reality. We do not see the world as it is; we see the world as we are. In other words, if you change the way you look at things, the things you look at will change.

Now ask yourself honestly. What do you believe, and how do you feel about people of other races? Your thoughts and feelings are a result of your perceptions, and your perceptions are the result of listening to your family, your culture and your society.

For example, if you happen to be white and do not have direct contact with black people, it's possible that you have a negative perception of black people because of the media and your family. Here is a case in point. In several cases of white police officers killing black men, they often say they felt threatened by the black men even if they didn't have a weapon, weren't aggressive or resisting arrest. So why did they feel threatened? They felt threatened because their perception of black men is all black men are angry and violent. And where did that perception come from? Primarily from the media, which disproportionately shows black men as being angry and violent. There is no scientific evidence supporting the idea that black men are inherently more violent than other men. The primary reason black men are perceived as violent is the disproportionate amount of news stories featuring black men and violence.

If you happen to be black and do not have direct contact with white people, it's possible that you have a negative perception of white people because of the media and your family. Case in point, you may have concluded that all white people are racists based on this country's history of racism and discrimination. Or maybe you watch conservative television that constantly promotes white supremacy and implies that people of color are inferior. It is quite possible that someone in your family may have experienced some form of racism, and they convinced you that all white people are racists.

If you happen to be a part of any minority group, you may have a perception that you are less than and inferior to people in the majority, which happen to be white people. Why would you accept this perception? Because the Rollercoaster I mentioned has conditioned you to believe that it's true. For example, the media-generated perception about Hispanics is that they are all illegal aliens coming to America to take our jobs. Do you remember what our former president of the United States of America said about people from Mexico? *"They are not our friend, believe me, they're bringing drugs. They're bringing crime. They're rapists. And some, I assume, are good people."* These were his words!

When the president of the United States says things like this on international television, do you not think it will create a negative perception of Hispanics in general? Of course, it did!

The key to embracing diversity is to be willing to challenge your perceptions about people who may look different and be different from you. This will take rigorous honesty on your part, and it may not be easy. Still, you can rest assured if you are courageous enough to challenge the deepest held thoughts and feelings you have about people who appear different from you, I can assure you that your life will only be enriched and you will become happier.

Are you willing to embrace diversity and change your perception of people who may be different from you? If so, let me share something that might help.

Some people believe the way to do this is with tolerance. Tolerance can be defined as *"the ability or willingness to tolerate something, in particular the existence of opinions or behavior that one does not necessarily agree with."*

I would like to suggest that a more effective way to do this is with acceptance. For me, tolerance has somewhat negative energy to it. A person may decide to "tolerate" someone, but they can still be angry or dislike that person deep down inside. On the other hand, acceptance, which can be defined as *"the act of accepting something or someone: the fact of being accepted,"* carries completely different energy. I can completely disagree with someone and still acknowledge their point of view. Therefore, there is no negative energy attached to it. When I know what my truth is and someone shares a different truth, by accepting that their truth is different from mine, I do not reject my truth. I simply accept their truth is different from mine. This is acceptance.

Now ask yourself these questions:

Can you accept someone who practices a different religion than you do?

Can you accept someone who has a different sexual orientation than you?

Can you accept someone who is a different race than you?

Can you accept someone with a different political affiliation than you?

Can you accept someone who comes from a different socio-economic level than you?

The answer to each of these questions is yes. All you have to do is make a conscious choice to accept people for who they are and choose not to judge or condemn people who may look different and believe differently than you do. To do this, you must be willing to engage with people different from you. You can do this by being willing to ask someone of a different race out to lunch. You can attend a church which is a different religion from your own. You can attend a gathering of the LGBTQ community. You can engage in a conversation with someone who shares different political views than you.

Of course, this won't be easy. It will probably be extremely uncomfortable. But that is the good news because there is no growth without discomfort, and if you are committed to your growth, you must become comfortable being uncomfortable.

This book intends to help you grow, and if you've gotten this far into it, then I'm certain you're committed to your growth. So always remember to embrace diversity in all of its forms, and you can build an extraordinary life.

"There are not enough problems for all of the solutions we already have."

— **Jurrian Kamp**
**Publisher of Kamp Solutions magazine.**

# CHAPTER 9
## Embrace Technology

I F YOU ASK most people if they are optimistic or pessimistic about the future in general, I believe most people would say they are pretty pessimistic. If you pay attention to mainstream media, it should be easy to understand their reasons for pessimism. We are constantly bombarded with negative images and stories that perpetuate the idea that the world is falling apart and headed down a path of destruction.

Contrary to mainstream media, I believe there are plenty of reasons for optimism and I personally believe there has never been a

better time to be alive on the planet than right now. There are two primary reasons for my optimism. First, I believe in a Divine Intelligence that created this Universe, and it is perfect, and second, I believe in technology. To clarify what I mean, I believe there are two types of technology. There is technological technology, and there is a human technology.

Human technology is the result of human evolution. Human beings are still evolving in consciousness, and this is what drives human technology. For example, therapy could be considered a form of human technology. A therapist is trained to implement strategies to help people overcome emotional and psychological challenges in their lives. In doing so, a person can learn to live a happier and healthier life. Participating in a seminar or workshop is also a form of human technology. It provides a systematic process of self-discovery which helps people become the best versions of themselves. This book falls under the category of human technology. It provides insights and wisdom which can support the reader in changing their mindset and attitude and helps them grow emotionally, intellectually, and spiritually.

Without question, human technology is more important than technological technology. We can have the most advanced technology in the world, but if the people using it aren't using it for the highest good of humanity, the technology will not be used to move humanity forward. My intention is to move humanity forward, so to do that, I have dedicated my life to sharing human technology.

Since the primary focus of this book has been dealing with human technology, I want to use this chapter to talk about the second reason for my optimism about the future, which is technological technology.

Simply stated, I Love Technology! I have always been somewhat of a technology geek, and as I look at some of the advances we're making in technology, I am filled with optimism about the future for humanity. I'd like to share a few of the technological advances that are being made in the world today, and I hope that they will inspire you to become more optimistic about the future and, more importantly, challenge you to embrace some of these technologies to support you in living an extraordinary life.

## 1. The Internet

Not since the printing press has a technology come along that has changed the world profoundly. The Internet, in my opinion, is the greatest technological breakthrough the world has ever seen. Through the Internet, the world has become a connected global community. We are no longer restricted by racial and cultural boundaries or limited by geographical boundaries. In many ways, it has connected us as one human family with the ability to connect with and communicate with anyone, anywhere around the globe.

The Internet gives anyone with a computer or phone and an Internet connection the opportunity to learn anything about any subject, and in most cases, at absolutely zero cost. As the debate continues about the value of college education, it's important to note that the Internet gives anyone access to an infinite amount of knowledge for little or no cost. I'm reminded of this quote, "If someone doesn't want to learn, no one can make them, but if someone truly wants to learn, no one can stop them."

What's stopping you from learning what you need to know?

## 2. Electric/Autonomous Cars and Vehicles

Few things are more exciting to me than electric cars. I am fascinated by the technology, and the long-term benefits of electric cars should be cause for excitement and optimism for the future. First of all, electric cars are better for the environment. Since fully electric cars do not have an exhaust system, they do not have emissions; therefore, they do not pump any fumes into the air, which means cleaner air and fewer greenhouse gases.

Another advantage of electric cars is that they can be powered by renewable resources like solar, wind, and water power. Gasoline-powered cars are fueled by oil, which is a natural resource, but it isn't renewable.

Electricity is also cheaper than gas, and powering electric cars typically costs one-third the cost of gas-powered vehicles. Since electric cars have very few moving parts, there is less frequent maintenance and need for repairs. In addition, electric cars are much quieter than gas-powered cars and therefore will reduce noise pollution.

These are a few of the mechanical advantages of electric cars, but what really excites me about them is their ability to become self-driving. Although the technology is still in an infancy stage, rest assured that autonomous self-driving cars and vehicles are the waves of the future. According to *Business Insider* magazine, they predict that in the future, most people will no longer own cars because of electric rideshare companies that will be launching fleets of autonomous self-driving cars. It has also been predicted that traffic fatalities, DWIs, and insurance rates will drop as more electric vehicles become available.

Currently, every major car manufacturer is launching or developing an electric car, so rest assured electric cars are the future. The primary downside of electric cars is cost. Still, as more companies commit to electric vehicles, demand will drive the prices down and pretty soon, they will be available to everyone. The other obstacle for electric cars is range. Currently, the average range of an electric vehicle is approximately 200 miles per charge, but as battery technology improves, so will the vehicle range.

Speaking of cars, did you know there are now several companies offering flying cars? That's right! Flying cars! Cars that you can drive on the road and then fly through the air. They are predicting these will be widely available in less than 25 years. A couple of companies have already received FAA approval and have begun selling their flying vehicles.

I'm reminded of the cartoon back in my childhood called *The Jetsons*. It was a futuristic animated show back in the '60s, and now it appears that the show was simply a preview of what was to come.

Cars have come a long way since the first car in 1886, and I can't wait to see what's next.

## 3. Drones

What began as a toy for grownups has now evolved into a full-fledged industry that is changing the world for the better. Drones are being used to deliver medicines in places that are not readily accessible by car and are saving countless lives. They are being used to fight fires and track endangered species of animals. People are using them to launch businesses and to record vacations and weddings. Rescue workers use them to locate victims of natural disasters, and farmers use them to plant seeds and distribute pesticides and fertilizers.

There are even drone competitions where people compete for large purses of money by being the best drone pilot.

What's really impressive are the upcoming flying drone taxis, which are getting ready to be launched by several airline companies and ride-sharing companies like Uber. In the very near future, you will be able to call a flying drone taxi company and have them pick you up and whisk you away as easily as calling a cab.

## 4. Solar Energy

In a new report, the International Energy Agency (IEA) says solar is now the cheapest form of electricity for utility companies to build. Thanks to risk-reducing financial policies around the world, the agency says, and it applies to locations with both the most favorable policies and the easiest access to financing. The report underlines how important these policies are to encouraging the development of renewables and other environmentally forward technologies.

This is definitely good news for the planet. As more and more forms of renewable energy like solar are created, we move closer and closer to reversing global warming. While some people are against the so-called Green New Deal proposed by some politicians, the advancement of solar power and other forms of renewable energy are the keys to solving climate change. As solar technology continues to evolve and the prices continue to drop, it opens the door for innovative entrepreneurs to develop new technologies and business models that will create new industries and jobs for the future.

## 5. Artificial Intelligence

I am not a scientist and cannot explain exactly what artificial intelligence is and how it works, but I believe it has a major impact on the world. If you have ever used a smartphone or talked to an Alexa device, you have used artificial intelligence. Without most people realizing it, artificial intelligence has already become ubiquitous in society and rest assured we've only scratched the surface of what's coming. A simple way to look at AI is to imagine a library filled with thousands of books. Now imagine you have all the content from that library installed in a computer program. Now imagine that you have a question that you need to be answered, so you input the question into the computer and the computer is able to find the answer to your question. That sounds simple, right? You probably think any computer can do that, right? But here is where AI comes in. AI can process all the content in the library and cross-reference all of it and find the answer in less than five seconds. No matter what question you ask, if the information is available in the library, AI will find it and be able to give you your answer. As computing power increases, it's like going from a library with thousands of books to a library of millions of books and still being able to process the information in less than one second.

In 2016, the world's first artificially intelligent lawyer named ROSS was hired by a law firm named Baker & Hostetler. ROSS is a piece of artificial intelligence software that uses the supercomputing power of IBM Watson to sort through millions of lawbooks and court cases. It has proven effective, and more law firms are now investing in the technology.

AI can be programmed for any industry. Many insurance companies are now using AI to put together insurance quotes over the phone based on this type of technology and are doing it without any human input. The entire policy can be put together using only AI computers.

Of course, the biggest fear of AI comes from watching too many movies about it taking over the world. If you're a fan of the *Terminator* movies, you may remember Skynet. Skynet was an AI technology that became self-aware and then took over the world and produced a bunch of Terminator robots, which attempted to wipe out civilization.

I personally do not believe this will ever happen, but there are some valid concerns about AI that must be addressed. No matter what, AI is here to stay, and I believe it is positively impacting the world.

## 6. Robots

In the movie *I Robot* with Will Smith, Will plays a detective who is extremely skeptical about robots, and he takes on a murder case in which a robot kills its owner. In the movie, the robots were designed to be servants who were sworn to protect their owners, and they couldn't figure out why this one robot would commit a homicide. The robot accused of murder turned out to be very special and, unlike the other robots, it began to have human emotions and even vivid dreams. In the beginning, Will didn't trust the robot and believed it had committed the murder. But upon further investigation, he learned to trust the robot and was able to solve the case after realizing that the main computer with artificial intelligence had become self-aware and had programmed the robots to do whatever it wanted them to do. It then began programming the robots to take over the planet. The robot killed his owner because his owner made him do it because he knew it would be the only way to stop the AI computer from taking over the world. He knew how much Will hated robots, and he knew he would solve the case and figure everything out. With the help of the accused robot, Will was able to destroy the AI computer and reprogram the other robots, and he was able to save the world.

It is a very enjoyable movie, and at the same time, it perpetuates the idea that robots will turn against humanity and take over the world. So, let's look at the positive side of robots and robotics and remove some of the fear many people may have about the future.

First of all, I believe the biggest concern most people have about robots is that they will replace humans and take away jobs. Although some robotics might do that, I believe robotics will also create jobs. As robotic technology progresses, there will be a need for repair personnel, software engineers, programmers, and even designers. As we usher in the decade of robotics, I believe a new industry could develop that hasn't been thought of yet. Herein lies the reason why entrepreneurship is critical. It is necessary to work with robots and robotics to create new industries and job opportunities so that jobs lost to robots can be replaced with new and innovative job opportunities.

Now let's look at some of the benefits of robotics and how they are positively impacting the world.

Have you ever used or seen robotic vacuum cleaners? These miniature robots are programmed to go around your house and vacuum your floors for you. Based on some reviews I've read, they actually do a pretty good job and based on their popularity, you can be sure that there will be new and better ones on the horizon.

One of the fastest-growing segments of robotics is robot-assisted surgeries for doctors. One of the most popular methods is called the da Vinci Surgical System. It allows surgeons to perform minimally invasive surgery with the help of robotic arms. The machine consists of four thin robotic arms inserted into strategically placed incisions just one to two centimeters long. The surgeon operates while seated at a console unit, using hand and foot controls and a 3D high-definition view of the surgical field. It can simulate an open surgical environment without the physical trauma of large incisions. The da Vinci System enables surgeons to perform even the most complex and delicate procedures through small, precise incisions.

One of the coolest robot companies is called Boston Dynamics, and they build a wide variety of different types of robots. They built a humanoid type robot called Atlas, which is the world's most dynamic humanoid robot and is designed to take the place of humans in a wide variety of environments. (You have to see it to believe it, so be sure to check out their website at www.bostondynamics.com) They can walk, run, roll over, and lift objects just like humans. You will be amazed when you see it doing gymnastics and jumping over objects.

They also have a robot called Spot, and it's like a robotic dog. It walks around on four legs and can be programmed to perform a wide variety of tasks. There was a video of one that had an iPad attached to it, and it was going around a hospital, and the doctor was interacting with patients to prevent the spread of the Covid virus. The patient could see the doctor and vice versa, and they were able to communicate as if the doctor was actually in the room.

It was pretty cool to watch.

One of the most realistic and intelligent robots is a robot named Sophia by a company called Hanson Robotics. Sophia uses the most advanced AI of any robot, and she can engage in real conversations with a human being. She can sense facial expressions and even understand human emotions. She has self-learning capabilities and can be programed to build simple electronics. She is so intelligent that in 2015, Saudi Arabia granted her citizenship in their country, and she is the first robot to be recognized as a citizen. Do a Google search and watch her in action; she's pretty remarkable.

Speaking of female robots, did you know there are also robot sex

Chapter 9: Embrace Technology

dolls? As creepy as that might seem, it's true. There are very realistic robots designed not only to have sex with but also to learn how to communicate with humans and develop relationships with them. The AI within them helps them learn things like your mood, your favorite movie or color, and they can remember these things and communicate with you about them. Supposedly, their skin is supposed to be very realistic, and they have simulated heartbeats and warm skin. As creepy as that sounds, and I would never want to have sex with a robot, I must admit that I am intrigued by the technology and would love to see one.

Overall, I believe robots will positively contribute to society. These are just a few examples of what they can do, but it doesn't scratch the surface of robotic potential for the future.

## 7. 3D Printing

Of all the technology on this list, 3D printing has the potential to have the biggest impact on the world. A 3D printer is a machine that can "print" different materials to create an unlimited amount of products and items. Starting with the basics, you can take a roll of plastic and insert it into the machine. You then build the item using a software program on the computer. Once you've built the 3D model on the machine, you simply press "print" and the machine takes the plastic and begins layering it until it builds whatever item you programmed into it.

Currently, scientists are developing ways to 3D print human body parts. They have already perfected things like human ears, and they predict they will be able to 3D print human hearts in the future. Imagine the possibilities with this technology. What if they are able to 3D print human lungs, kidneys, or hearts? Imagine how many lives could be saved every year with this technology.

Another amazing use of 3D technology is construction. Companies can now 3D print an entire house, including plumbing and electrical in just a few days made from concrete. As the technology improves and costs begin to fall, just imagine going to third-world countries and being able to 3D print entire villages in just a few months. In just a few years, this could become a reality. There is a company in China called WinSun Decoration Design Engineering Co. They currently have the record for the tallest 3D printed structure, a five-story apartment complex. They are also known for 3D printing 10 complete houses in 24 hours and have even built an 11,840 ft. mansion.

Believe it or not, 3D printed cars are a reality.

Although you may not be able to find 3D printed cars at your local car dealership just yet, some very interesting concepts out there do a great job of presenting the possibilities of 3D printing in the automotive industry. They even represent the first steps toward mass-produced 3D printed cars. Don't be surprised if you see a story about 3D printed automobiles. They are already being printed, and they range from tiny economical mini cars to exotic style supercars.

The future for 3D printing is extremely bright. Companies are only limited by their imaginations of what can be printed. This is a technology I will definitely be following to keep up with the infinite possibilities that are being brought forth.

## 8. Gene Editing

One of the most fascinating and controversial technologies is a process called gene editing. It's called CRISPR, and it has the potential to change the world for the better. Here is some information I copied from the website www.newscientist.com:

*CRISPR is a technology that can be used to edit genes and, as such, will likely change the world.*

*The essence of CRISPR is simple: it's a way of finding a specific bit of DNA inside a cell. After that, the next step in CRISPR gene editing is usually to alter that piece of DNA. However, CRISPR has also been adapted to do other things too, such as turning genes on or off without altering their sequence. CRISPR technology also has the potential to transform medicine, enabling us to not only treat but also prevent many diseases.*

In other words, imagine being able to identify a genetically diseased gene like sickle cell and being able to remove that gene, repair the DNA, and thereby remove the disease. WOW!

Chapter 9: Embrace Technology

The implications of this technology are mind-blowing. It has the potential of one day being able to cure a wide range of diseases.

## 9. Space Exploration

In January of 2004, NASA landed two rover vehicles on Mars. They were called Spirit and Opportunity. Their primary goal was to find out whether or not Mars ever had water on the planet. The mission was supposed to last only 90 days, but the rovers exceeded expectations because the Spirit rover lasted six years, and the Opportunity rover lasted 14 years. The mission confirmed the existence of water on the planet, and without question, it was a huge success.

In September of 2016, NASA launched the Osiris-Rex spacecraft to travel more than 200 million miles to rendezvous with an asteroid named Bennu. It took two years for the spacecraft to get there, and once there, it was able to retrieve some soil samples, which would be returned to earth.

On December 25th 2021, Nasa launched the James Webb Space Telescope. It is the most powerful telescope ever launched into space; its greatly improved infrared resolution and sensitivity will allow it to view objects too old, distant, and faint for the Hubble Space Telescope to detect. This is expected to enable a broad range of investigations across the fields of astronomy and cosmology, such as observations of first stars and the formation of first galaxies and detailed atmospheric characterization of potentially habitable exoplanets.

These are just three major examples of the ingenuity and innovation of America's space program. However, they only scratch the surface of what's ahead in space exploration. Here are a few other examples of what to look forward to.

### Asteroid Mining

There is an asteroid called 16 Psyche, located in an asteroid belt between Mars and Jupiter. NASA estimates that the minerals on that asteroid are worth 10 quadrillion dollars. That's a 1 with 19 zeros behind it. That's more than the entire economy of Earth. I'm not sure if they plan on trying to retrieve any of the minerals, but several companies are now launching asteroid mining projects. It will be interesting to see if this new industry discovers new minerals or substances that may be beneficial to humanity and helps create new technology.

## Moon Mining

Moon Express is a company owned by Naveen Jain. It was the first company to receive U.S. government approval to send a robotic spacecraft beyond traditional Earth orbit and to the Moon. Naveen said, "Our robotic spacecraft systems will collapse the cost of access to the Moon, introduce a new commercial paradigm for government missions, democratize lunar research and exploration, and blaze the trail for commercial space transportation and exploration beyond Earth's orbit."

## Space Travel Tourism

Virgin Galactic is now offering sub-orbital flights. Customers will be able to enter the lower fringes of space and float in zero gravity and take in spectacular views of our amazing planet. Tickets start at $250,000, but if it works and takes off, rest assured there will be more competition, which will definitely drive down the cost. Sign me up baby! I would love to go.

Some people believe space exploration is a waste of money and we should focus on social problems on Earth before we begin exploring space. I completely disagree. It is absolutely imperative that we have a space program because it allows us to learn about space and gives us an opportunity to develop a contingency plan just in case Earth becomes uninhabitable. Who knows what will happen in the future, so why not begin thinking about worst-case scenarios so we are prepared just in case?

As an optimist, these technologies give me a reason for hope and excitement. I have great faith in humanity, and ultimately, I believe we will rise above all of our challenges. Technology can lead the way, but we must remember not to place it before our humanity.

The key is for you to be willing to embrace technology and use it to improve your life. I'm well aware that many people do not like change, and being willing to embrace it can be difficult. But rest assured, if you are committed to creating an extraordinary life, you will have to learn some new things and gain some new skills. Alvin Toffler once stated, "The functional illiterate of the 21$^{st}$ century will not be those who can't read or write, the functional illiterate will be those who are unwilling to learn, unlearn, and relearn."

Remember this quote from personal development expert Tony Robbins. "The key to your success is CANI. Constant and Never-ending Improvement." Embrace CANI and technology, and I can assure you that your life can become extraordinary.

Do not be afraid of technology. Embrace it and find ways you can use it to improve the quality of your life.

Always remember, people first; technology second!

*I slept and dreamt that life was joy. I awoke and saw that life was service. I acted and behold, service was joy.*

**— Rabindranath Tagore**

# CHAPTER 10
## Embrace Being In Service

As we come to the end of this book, I'm reminded of a beautiful quote by the poet Rumi. *"Let yourself be silently drawn by the stronger pull of what you really love."* Throughout this book, I've mentioned there is a Divine Intelligence that permeates the Universe, and you have direct access to that intelligence. I will assert that *"the stronger pull of what you really love"* is actually Divine Intelligence. The pull you feel is the God in you seeking to express itself through you, as you.

Take a moment and think about how and why you've come across this particular book at this particular time in your life. Were you dealing with adversity and looking for ways to deal with it? Did you "accidentally" find it while perusing a social media site? Or maybe you ran across an article about the book and felt compelled to check it out. Or maybe a close friend or relative recommended it to you.

No matter how you came across the book, rest assured, it wasn't an accident. A part of you attracted this book to yourself because there is a message within this book that you were supposed to get. Did you get it? Did this book provide you with any insights to support you in creating an extraordinary life?

I'd like to share another quote that shares a divine truth which speaks directly to my point.

> *"Fortunately, some are born with spiritual immune systems that sooner or later give rejection to the illusory worldview grafted upon them from birth through social conditioning. They begin sensing that something is amiss, and start looking for answers. Inner knowledge and anomalous outer experiences show them a side of reality others are oblivious to, and so begins their journey of awakening. Each step of the journey is made by following the heart instead of following the crowd and by choosing knowledge over the veils of ignorance."*
>
> — Henri Bergson

I believe you were attracted to this book because you have begun your journey of awakening. I believe a part of you needed to hear this message, and fortunately, you listened to that part of yourself and decided to read this book. I believe you are ready to wake up!

Did the book help you wake up? Have you gained some insights that will help you along your journey of awakening so that your life can become extraordinary? If your answer is yes, you must answer this question:

Do you believe it's possible for you to create an extraordinary life?

Rest assured, the answer to that question is an emphatic yes! You have everything you need already inside of you to create the life of your dreams. It all begins with your belief that it's possible. It does not matter how old you are, what your skin color is, how much education you have, who your parents are, or what country you're from. Your beliefs create your reality, so the first thing you must do is simply believe that an extraordinary life is possible for you.

It is up to you to decide what extraordinary might look like, but rest assured, it can happen if you believe it's possible. It all begins with a single belief.

Take a moment and think about my life story. I am a young black male born in the inner-city projects of Corpus Christi, Texas, to a single mother with six kids. We were the poster children for poverty back in the sixties. I dropped out of high school in the eleventh grade and never went to college. I climbed the corporate ladder at the age of twenty-three years old and lived the American Dream. That dream turned into a nightmare at twenty-nine years old as I experienced divorce, bankruptcy, foreclosure, depression, and being homeless for two years living out of my car. Despite all of these adversities, I was able to rebuild my life, and it has become extraordinary.

How was I able to do this? I simply believed it was possible and was willing to do whatever it took to make my life extraordinary. Was it easy? Absolutely not! It was painful, difficult, scary, challenging, and confusing, yet I was committed to making it happen, and I did. If I can do it, I'm certain you can also.

So how would you define an extraordinary life? What would your life look like if it were extraordinary? Of course, extraordinary will mean different things to different people. Still, I can assure you that if your life is to become extraordinary, it will have to include these four components.

Inner Peace, Dynamic Health, Great Relationships, and Financial Abundance.

Inner peace arises from knowing who you truly are, your qualities and values. It comes from having a connection to a power greater than yourself and being comfortable in your own skin. This is why chapter two is so important. You must be willing to embrace who you truly are by doing your inner work and making peace with your past in order to truly experience inner peace. Inner peace also comes from having intimacy and connection with a power greater than yourself. You get to choose how you connect to the Divine, but you must have some type of daily practice that keeps you connected. I highly recommend you commit to daily meditation practice because I don't know of any other way to connect intimately with Divine Intelligence. Prayer is also a powerful way to have inner peace. It's been said that prayer is talking to God, and meditation is listening to God, so be sure to do both.

Dynamic health is the result of taking good care of your physical body. This means being able to physically do whatever you'd like to do without unnecessary discomfort. It means watching your weight and getting annual checkups to ensure your body operates at an optimal level. It means exercising, eating right and abstaining from illegal drugs and overindulgence in alcohol. It means feeling good physically!

Relationships are the glue that holds our lives together, so it's important to create great relationships. Having great friends and support networks are an integral part of creating an extraordinary life. Choosing the right life partner should be a high priority in your life because it is the most important relationship for you to have, so be sure to choose that person wisely to share your life with.

Financial abundance simply means that you have enough money so you no longer have to be stressed out about it. Therefore, it's incumbent upon you to figure out a way to bring in enough money to remove that stress, and more importantly, you have to learn to make sure that you have more money coming in than you have going out. Only you can decide what financial abundance means to you, but the key is asking yourself how much you worry about money in your life. If you are constantly worrying about your money, you are not financially abundant no matter how much you make. When you are able to stop stressing about money, then you will be financially abundant.

Once you balance these four things, Inner Peace, Dynamic Health, Great Relationships, and Financial Abundance, there is only one other thing you must do for your life to become extraordinary.

You must be willing to be in service to humanity in some way.

Being in service to humanity simply means you are willing to share your unique gifts and talents with the world to help make it a better place. This doesn't mean that you have to become Mother Theresa or Gandhi. It simply means that you somehow positively impact the life of another human being.

I want to close this book with another way to look at being in service. I wrote about this in my previous book titled Brothers Are You Listening? It is a perfect way to close out the final chapter of this book.

Without question, God's greatest creation is the human body. Jesus said, "Tear down the temple of God and I will rebuild it in three days!" The temple he spoke of was his physical body. I believe that the human body is simply a microcosm of the universe. (1 Corinthians 12:14-27) states:

> *Now the body is not made up of one part but of many. If the foot should say, 'Because I am not a hand, I do not belong to the body,' it would not for that reason cease to be part of the body. And if the ear should say, 'Because I am not an eye, I do not belong to the body,' it would not for that reason cease to be part of the body. If the whole body were an eye, where would the sense of hearing be? If the whole body were an ear, where would the sense of smell be? But, in fact, God has arranged the parts in the body, every one of them, just as he wanted them to be. If they were all one part, where would the body be? As it is, there are many parts, but one body. The eye cannot say to the hand, "I don't need you!" And the head cannot say to the feet, "I don't need you!" On the contrary, those parts that seem to be weaker are indispensable, and the parts that we think are less honorable, we treat with special honor. And the unpresentable parts are treated with special modesty, while our presentable parts need no special treatment.*
>
> *But God has combined the members of the body and has given a great honor to the parts that lacked it so that there should be no division in the body, but its parts should have equal concern for each other. If one part suffers, every part suffers with it: if one part is honored, every part rejoices with it. Now you are the body of Christ, and each one of you is a part of it.*

I believe this passage substantiates my belief.

Take a moment and think about your body. It is the greatest miracle in the world. Think about how your organs are perfectly placed within. Your heart, lungs, kidneys, intestines, spleen, gall bladder, and your brain are all strategically placed within the framework of God's greatest creation.

If you cut yourself, the cells within automatically know what has to take place to heal the wound. You don't have to think to yourself, "Cells, I need you to fix this cut." The cells do this automatically. When a person exercises, the muscles automatically know that they have to grow to compensate for the extra strength needed to lift the weights. The harder you work the human body, the stronger it becomes. Have you ever really thought about the miracle healing power of the human body? If you break a bone, how does it heal? Some people think, "I go to a doctor, they put a cast on it, and it's healed." That is true, but we need to take a closer look at the process. As I've mentioned, the internal cells automatically know what has to take place for the healing to occur. But how do the cells know this? Obviously, some Divine Intelligence is within the cells that direct them to do their particular duty.

This divine intelligence, I believe, is God.

It is that life-giving energy within the cells of every living creature that automatically knows what has to happen to heal a living organism.

Now take a moment and think about the earth. Imagine that the earth is just like your body. It has strategically placed organs which we call countries and millions of cells which we call people. Like your body, it is sometimes invaded by germs and diseases. Some of the diseases that attack the earthy body are Wars, Hatred, Racism, and Fear. Think about the war between Russia and Ukraine. Think of Ukraine as a kidney within the earth's body. The kidney was invaded by a germ called Vladimir Putin. This germ tried to take over the entire organ. As it made its initial attempt at taking over the organ, several other cells decided to be like the germ and started acting like it. Now we have a disease because the germ has started to multiply.

But because of the divine intelligence of the whole body, it had to start healing itself by sending out some good cells to get rid of the bad germs. Enter in NATO, and NATO brought together other countries that acted as the good cells within the earth's body and started the process of healing. I personally never condone wars; I simply wanted to use this analogy to let you see the big picture. The point is that you are a cell within the body of God. Like a cell within the human body, you have a specific purpose. That purpose is to heal the body.

Although the media would have you believe that the world is in total chaos, I would like to assert to you, at this time, that what is actually taking place is God's body is healing itself. I also believe that this healing process has begun to accelerate. As we continue to evolve as a human species, we will experience a new level of peace and understanding.

As a single cell in the body of God, when you choose to assist in healing the body, then you are in service. As I mentioned, that is the reason for our existence: to serve. Whenever you hear someone talk about the will of God, it simply means that they are doing their part in healing the body.

Another word for that divine healing power is Love. It is simply God in action directing you to your highest good to assist Divine Intelligence in healing its body. When a human being chooses to spread love unconditionally, he becomes the antidote for all illnesses. When we drink from that fountain of Love and spread that Love around, the body becomes filled with Love and ultimately becomes healed.

Throughout history, God has given certain cells the task of healing his body on a very large scale. I believe that Jesus was the ultimate healer. He tapped into that infinite well of Love and created a healing process that transcended all other great healing masters. Jesus was the ultimate cell in the body of God. But as He mentioned in (John 14:12) "I tell you the truth, anyone who has faith in me will do what I have been doing. He will do even greater things than these because I am going to the Father. And I will do whatever you ask in my name, so that the Son may bring glory to the Father."

That means that we all can heal just like He did. All we need to do is make a conscious effort to follow His teachings and the world will be healed. Most of us don't believe that we have that same power. I think it frightens us to think that we could do the things that Jesus did. But the truth is, we all have a voice to speak out in truth, and each one of us can contribute to the healing process. When I think about Dr. Martin Luther King Jr., I realize that he also tapped into that infinite well of love. Because of his commitment to non-violence, he showed us that he could move mountains with love. And he did. Rather than accept all the anger and hatred that surrounded him daily, he followed his heart and surrendered to God. He followed Jesus' lead to not try and defuse anger with anger, but with love. I realize that many people still believe we should fight fire with fire and retaliate with anger and hatred, but that only creates more of the same. Hatred and anger create disease within the body of God, and it only slows the healing process.

To assist in this process, we must first take an honest look at ourselves and see how we are participating in life at this particular moment. If you have read through this book, you may have noticed some areas in which you can make some changes within yourself that will assist in the healing of the planet. To heal, a cell must be healthy first. If it is contaminated, then it will only spread that contamination. Once you have become healthy, start spreading yourself around to assist other people in becoming healthy. As I mentioned, each human being is created the same. They simply have a different purpose. So, never try and compare yourself to other people; simply be the best you can be in all areas of your life. I promise you will be automatically doing your part in healing the planet.

If you are looking for some specific ways to assist in the healing of the planet, let me make a few suggestions.

First and foremost, learn to love yourself. I realize that this may come as a shock to some of you, but that is the key. Thirty years ago, if someone even mentioned the word love, I became uncomfortable and would accuse that person (if they were male) of being weak and overly sensitive. But if you ever experience true love on a deep, emotional, spiritual level the way I have over the past few years, you would definitely have a change of heart. You would also know what it feels like to experience heaven right here on earth.

Taking the time to understand ourselves first is the key to being happy. Next, I believe that a spiritual connection of some sort is essential. Remember, it doesn't matter what container you're drinking from; just make sure you're getting your spiritual thirst quenched. You have to make sure that you are tapping into that well daily. This is an absolute must. The more you drink, the more you get.

Make sure that you participate in something that uplifts you spiritually, not something that drags you down with guilt and negativity. If there is a Unity Church of Christianity in your area, you might consider giving it a try. Whatever you choose, make sure it makes you feel good. That's the difference between religion and spirituality. Spirituality feels great because you are tapping into that life-giving force of love. In some cases, religion is extremely uncomfortable because it pushes shame and condemnation on you, which goes against the true nature of who you are.

Give something back! We each have special gifts and talents that we should use to be in service to our Creator. Acknowledge those gifts and share them with someone. Whenever you're being creative, you're simply letting that infinite intelligence flow through you. If you love to sing, then start singing; if you love to dance, start dancing. Whatever you choose to do, do it with love and passion. Remember when you were a kid, and you weren't concerned about what people thought of you and would sing or dance at a moment's notice? You were simply expressing yourself, and it felt great. If you will be yourself and love what you do, then you are in service. For example, writing this book is a way of being in service. It allows me to not only share my experiences with you but hopefully empower you to take action and heal the planet. You don't have to write a book to give something back, although I suggest you consider it. We empower others to share their stories by sharing our positive uplifting stories. As soon as we start focusing on what's right instead of what's wrong, we will start creating more right things.

Giving back means spreading love. You can do that by smiling at a stranger or helping someone with a flat tire. You can donate a pint of blood or volunteer your services. Have you ever noticed how good it feels to give love unconditionally? Whenever you do that, you are simply expressing God. Maybe you're walking down the street and you give a homeless person a dollar without any thoughts of getting something in return. All of a sudden, something inside says, "Way to go!" My favorite is hugs. Of course, most men are extremely uncomfortable with this, but I love them, especially from my kids.

When was the last time you had a great hug? If more people hugged each other, we could melt away a lot of pain. Commit to love yourself and others, and do everything with love. When you do this, you will experience Heaven on Earth the way God intended.

Commit yourself to service.

I hope this book has provided some information and inspiration to assist you in being all you were created to be. You have to believe that you do have the power within you to live your dreams and enjoy a life filled with joy, peace and love. Whether you admit it or not, love is at the core of your being. You can choose to accept this, or you can continue to experience pain and emptiness in your life. I promise that the love and joy will beat the pain and sorrow any day. You don't have to pretend any longer; all you have to do is take action.

Commit to loving yourself, and you will be doing your part in healing the world.

# Bio

Coach Michael Taylor is an entrepreneur, author (11 books), motivational speaker, and radio show host who has dedicated his life to empowering men and women to reach their full potential. He knows first-hand how to overcome adversity and build a rewarding and fulfilling life, and he is sharing his knowledge and wisdom with others to support them in creating the life of their dreams.

He was featured in the bestselling book Motivational Speakers America with speaking legends Les Brown and Brian Tracey, and he is also an Amazon.com bestselling author. He has won numerous awards for his dynamic speaking style, and he has been featured on multiple radio and TV interviews across the country.

He is President & CEO of Creation Publishing Group, which is a company that specializes in creating programs and products that empower men and women to create extraordinary lives. He currently hosts three television channels on the Roku Television Network.

Most importantly, he has been blissfully married for 20 years to the woman of his dreams, and he is a proud father to three grown children and two grandchildren whom he is extremely proud of.

When he isn't writing or speaking, you'll find him checking out the latest movies or listening to old school 70s and 80s soul music and contemporary jazz.

He considers himself an irrepressible optimist with a passion for the impossible, and he believes there has never been a better time to be alive on this planet than right now.

www.coachmichaeltaylor.com

www.stssummit.com

www.joypassionprofit.com

www.adversityisyourgreatestally.com

www.creationpublishing.com

www.anewconversationwithmen.com

www.shatteringblackmalestereotypes.com

Contact us:

Email: mtaylor@coachmichaeltaylor.com

Phone: 877-255-3588

www.ingramcontent.com/pod-product-compliance
Lightning Source LLC
Chambersburg PA
CBHW050414120526
44590CB00015B/1963